I REMEMBER,
I REMEMBER

I REMEMBER,
I REMEMBER

LAYONA GLENN
with Charlotte Hale Smith

FLEMING H. REVELL COMPANY
Old Tappan, New Jersey

All Scripture quotations are from the *King James Version of the Bible*

To my dear friends,

John and Estelle Ledbetter

Contents

I REMEMBER,
I REMEMBER

1.
1866

ON MARCH 8, 1866 on our Yellow River plantation a few miles beyond Conyers, Georgia, I doubt you could tell there ever had been a war.

The hands had begun their spring plowing. The Yellow River ran high with rain water and melted snow, and the hills with their greening pine, sweet gum, oak and tulip poplar trees looked like you'd flung a delicate new shawl around their shoulders.

Dad always said I picked a fine day to be born, and a fine place. He called our old home place "God's country." My birth meant a really special joy for him and Mama, for I was their first baby born after Dad came home from the War Between the States.

My father never would talk much about the war. As a surgeon in the Confederate Army under General John H. Morgan's command in Virginia, I expect he saw more than he cared to tell. Anyhow he came on home, and just one day shy of eleven months after the chaos ended, I was born.

I opened my eyes not on ruin and destruction but on peace and plenty, though it's hard to believe *any* Georgia baby did that year. Only forty miles to the west of us Atlanta still reeked of smoke long months after General William T. Sherman put that city to the torch. Within ten miles of us other towns had suffered Sherman's famous march to the sea—endless lines of blue-clad soldiers had burned some farms, and looted others.

Grandpa and the hands took all our cattle and drove them into the canebrake. They hid there for three days until they felt sure Sherman's men had gone. Even patients from the Confederate Army Hospital at nearby Covington limped into the woods to hide, or were carried there on stretchers.

But that kind of terror was over and done. My birthday found Dad and Mama praising God for my father's safe return, for His mercifully sparing our home and its beautiful acres, and for protecting Mama and the five older children through the long war.

Dad named me Susan Layona Glenn. My parents took great stock in the long, fancy names so stylish then. They hung family names like garlands on their children: Sarah Eulalia Glenn, Joshua Estelle Nunnally Glenn, Wingfield Mapp Overton Glenn, Mary Georgia Glenn, John Garland Foster Glenn; then came me, followed by William Ivanhoe Nichols Glenn and Allen Turner Glenn.

Of course we took on nicknames. We had to! Dad called

Mary Georgia "Minnie Bug". My first sister's name was shortened to "Eula", and brother Estelle was called "Dutch," and they dubbed me "Peg."

But Dad called me Layona, an Indian word he learned from Will Rogers' father and two uncles, who were Cherokee Indians. The four used to hunt deer at night. They'd shine a light in the deer's eyes, which at a long distance would reflect from one eye to the other like a bar. When they reached a certain distance the light would reflect from each eye separately and they could shoot the animal squarely between the eyes.

However, when an Indian called out, "layona!" nobody shot.

The word *layona* indicates the young of the deer, the fawn. Dad said the very sound of the word seemed to protect the little animal. He took a notion, and gave it to me. It has given me a world of trouble: explaining the meaning, for one thing, and then getting folks to pronounce the word right. You say *Lah-yo-nah.*

My first clear memory on this earth is of something that happened one hundred and one years ago, yet I recall it with absolute clarity. I wasn't quite two years old, because this happened before my next brother was born, and I was exactly two years older than he.

A young student preacher from the Methodist seminary at nearby Oxford, Georgia, was visiting us. Preachers in training used to love to come to our farm to hunt, fish and

13

spend the weekend, and they were welcome at our house. This one, a young man named LaPrade, was playing with me. They all liked to play with the baby. I had LaPrade on the living room floor and I was up on his back, riding him like a horse.

We were racing in fine style until Mama whirled into the room, stamped her foot, and said, "Brother LaPrade, get up from there! You are *ruining* that child!"

Dad and Mama, infinitely loving as they were, didn't believe in spoiling children. Our family knew about industry, because anything we needed had to be made on the place. Our plantation sustained everyone on it.

There was no school out in the country, so Dad hired a governess to live with us and teach his children. She also taught the six children of his friend Dr. Bryan, who lived nearby, as well as all the tenant children.

Our parents didn't leave all our education to the governess, however. For example, Dad, who was a great reader, directed our reading. We'd come to his room each evening, sit around the huge stone fireplace, and while some of the children read aloud, the rest of us seeded cotton.

I still can almost smell the piney log fragrance of the wood fire, and taste the walnuts we cracked on the hearth. We opened so many nuts on Dad's broad old hearthstone that at last a little depression appeared there, a naturally handy place to crack more nuts!

Near the fireplace, Dad kept a big atlas that opened out

two feet wide, and a big *Webster's Dictionary* on a stand. While the older children took turns reading, the rest of us listened. Since Dad knew we couldn't *just* listen without fidgeting, he gave us something to do with our fingers.

Our father took particular pains to conserve the best seed each year so as to improve his cotton crops. When he stuck a stob beside a stalk of cotton, the hands knew they were to take particular pains with that cotton and see that nobody picked it.

Dad would select the bolls carefully, and at night we children were set to picking out seeds by hand. I remember the smooth feel of the seeds, the sound of a child's voice reading aloud, a fire popping, and the comfortable sounds of apples being crunched and nuts being cracked. When someone read a word you didn't know, you'd raise your hand to ask what it meant. Then you'd go to the dictionary to hunt up the word and read it to the others.

That way each child built a large vocabulary. My own has been compared to Woodrow Wilson's.

The simple fun and the rich companionship of those evenings linger in my mind, so do the books. Almost always the books were about travel—wonderful favorite stories, like Mark Twain's *Innocents Abroad.*

Before eight o'clock came, and bed time, we'd kneel before the fire as my father read from the Holy Bible and prayed. We listened quietly, heads bowed; and as we listened, we picked out cotton seed!

I Remember, I Remember

We children considered our parents the best in the world, and we knew we had the most wonderful house to be found. I still think so. I believe any millionaire today gladly would pay a million dollars for that house.

It was a log house, built of peeled logs about ten inches in diameter. Inside the walls had been covered with lathes and plaster, and the ceilings were high and the rooms exceptionally large. The wonderful thing about the house, I thought, was its space.

The two big front rooms measured eighteen by twenty feet and were separated by a fifteen-foot hall. Behind them was the dining room, which was twenty feet square, and at the rear was the kitchen. Triple-sash windows went clear to the floor and opened onto the front verandah outside.

You never saw more beautiful land than that which surrounded our lovely old house. There was a pretty, high hill with the Yellow River flowing beyond it, and Bald Rock gleaming across the river. We had our mill there, Bald Rock Mill, with a water race that brought water down from the hills and over a huge wheel which furnished power.

The wheel ran our sawmill and turning lathe, where the furniture was made, and the mill that ground our flour. Three acres of level land faced the mill sites, and two enormous water oaks framed the picture. Beyond these, you could discover the blacksmith's shop.

Dad's office was located near the house. We were supposed to stay away from there, but I always hung around

16

Dad, wanting to "help" him, and he pretty much let me.

That plantation by the old Yellow River was our world, brim full of good life. America was young then, not quite ninety years old when I was born, and our little corner of the world remained unspoiled. Here we children played and fought and dreamed and learned and enjoyed one another. If I had to choose the exact center of our world, I'd say Dad and Mama's room.

It served as the living room too, you know. That's where we'd gather around the fire in the evenings, and in my memory I still see the flickering firelight shining on the various faces as we read and worked. Always I see that room at night, with the family there, and the lamplight gleaming on the great stone fireplace where we hung the long row of Christmas stockings, and shining on the tall glass-fronted book cases where Mama kept her four-volume *King James Version of the Holy Bible* from which I learned my ABC's. And I see Dad's bed, tall and solid, and six feet square.

Beneath it, they kept a trundle bed just as large as Dad's. He and Mama pulled it out each evening and bedded me there, with my two little brothers. Oh, it was the coziest place in the world, Dad and Mama's room—the place where our family was happiest.

It stayed that way until the year I turned seven. That year Mama got so sick that even I knew it was bad.

Dad tried everything he knew. He even sent to Augusta

for the president of the Georgia Medical Academy. There in front of that fireplace, with the family at evening prayer, Dad made Mama's recovery a matter of faith. Night after night he prayed, begging God to raise his Mary up.

Mama died anyhow. They laid her out on Dad's bed. I knew what had happened, and understood that my mother was gone. I sat down beside the bed and began to cry for my mother, and a neighbor woman swooped in and got me by the arm.

"Run on out yonder and play," she commanded me. "She don't know what she's crying about," she told the others.

But I did, I did! I'd never felt anything like the hatred that rose up in me then, and I'm afraid I never exactly forgave that woman.

I remember my mother. I remember her going.

2.
Childhood

WHEN MAMA DIED, Dad just went wild. He threw up his faith in God and everything else and took to drinking.

He and Mama had grown up together and had loved one another from the beginning of time. Neither of them could remember when they decided they'd be married some day. When they reached their teen years, when boys and girls began to go together, Wink and Mary always paired off.

Everybody knew John Wingfield Glenn and Susan Mary Ann Nunnally never could consider having any other sweethearts. The two remained inseparable. Until Mama died, they had been apart only twice in all their lives.

The first time was when Dad went off to medical school in Augusta, and Mama enrolled in finishing school in Madison. Oh, the parting must have seemed cruel! In those days, boys and girls in school never were allowed to correspond.

Grandpa Nunnally, however, told Mama's principal that she was to be permitted to write once a week to Wink, and the letters needn't be censored, so they had the consolation of correspondence. Then my parents married and never again were separated in this life, except for the war years.

Although I wouldn't consider Dad and Mama unusually devout, they were good Christian people. Our family had prayers at breakfast, and prayers and Bible reading at night. Our parents took us kids to church regularly; church-going simply was part of the week's performance, and not to be missed. We got up early, got ready, and walked the three miles to the First Methodist Church at Mount Tabor, where both of our parents assumed leadership.

In those days families observed the Sabbath. We never cooked on Sunday. We cooked all Sunday's food the day before, and only made coffee on Sunday mornings.

In some ways, Dad's reaction to Mama's death didn't change this calm world as much as you might think. Things were different, terribly different, yet much of our life stayed the same as always. The servants made sure of this.

The slaves had been freed by the time I was born, but refused to leave, and, in fact had no place to go. We had wonderful help on the place. Before the war, Dad never permitted our people to be sold or bought except in case of marriage. If one of his slaves fell in love with somebody else's slave over yonder, my father either would buy or sell.

Aunt Sarah, who grew up with my mother and was her maid from their childhood days, fell in love and wanted to

20

marry, but she refused to leave Mama. My father paid two prices to Judge Floyd for Charley, who became Sarah's husband. Charley was a fine blacksmith and all sorts of a fine workman, so Dad paid a high price for him. My grandpa Glenn, who was a Methodist preacher, married them.

We loved those loyal people who did everything they could for us kids after Mama died.

Nevertheless, the first months without Mama were bad. Little as I was, I understood the pain and despair in Dad's heart, and though our family held together in our accustomed routines, I could feel a terrible difference in our lives. Mama died in September. As the weeks wore on, my little brothers and I began to wonder whether or not Santa Claus would come to see little children who had no mother.

On Christmas morning we opened our eyes with fear and trembling, almost afraid to hope. At first we didn't see a thing; we knew Santa Claus must have passed us by.

Then we spied a great big box sitting in the middle of the floor. Dad, who had no heart to fix Christmas for us, had shoved things into the box, pushed it into the middle of the room, and allowed us to discover it there.

That year I thought I ought to take on more responsibility. I began to look after my little brothers who were just five and three when we lost our mother. I also looked after the cook's two children, the same ages as my little brothers, and inseparable playmates. Young as I was, I held myself completely responsible for that flock of babies.

We had a big old dog named Don, and we had taught him to retrieve things. One day when the Yellow River was high, we began to throw sticks in the water so this dog could jump in and bring them out. The baby fetched a huge stick, nearly as big as he was, and proceeded to drag it toward the water. Suddenly the bank caved in beneath his little feet. Into the river he went!

"Get him, Don!" I screamed.

The river ran ten feet deep at that point. There were no grownups within shouting distance. I screamed again and again.

Don jumped instantly, seized the child by the shoulder of his little shirt, and held his blond head above the water.

Don swam strongly, towing his precious load. The other children followed me along the high river bank, until at last we reached a place where it met the road. Then I waded out to meet Don and take his burden from him.

I don't know that Dad ever knew about that incident— seems to me I never mentioned it!

I extended to my father, too, my new seven-year-old sense of responsibility. Of course I needed him, and somehow I sensed that he needed me. I took to hanging around his office, making those bread pills he often used. You'd take a little tad of bread, work it and work it, and when it commenced to look like a pill, you'd roll it in sugar so it would taste like one. Dad said lots of times people didn't need medicine—they just needed attention.

Despite his disapproval, I often managed to be present when Dad's more interesting cases arrived. He'd get busy and I'd slip in where I had no business to be. Dad's work fascinated me, and I thought I wanted to become a doctor. One day,when I was eight, I decided to begin my practice.

I had watched Dad operate on one of our hired men who had a queer little outgrowth at the knuckle joint of both fifth fingers. (The beginnings of a sixth finger is what it was.) Every member of his family had that same strange birth accident, and sometimes Dad would remove those flaps of skin so another of the children could have normal hands.

I saw Dad perform one of the operations and decided then and there that I could do it too. Dad simply tied a string right tight around that extra flesh, clipped it off, then cauterized it. It looked easy enough.

I got one of the children who still had those little toots extending from his small fingers. I tied that thing good and hard and tight clipped it off with scissors, cauterized it with aluminum phosphate, and it worked fine.

When I did the other hand, however, I must have cut too close to the string. Whatever I did, it bled; the blood just shot. I knew I'd have to face up to Dad.

I led my little patient into the office and Dad took two or three little stitches in his hand and dismissed him. But he didn't dismiss me! He put me up on his lap and gave me the once-over! He let me know I must not practice medicine without a license.

Even when Dad was drinking, mealtimes stayed pretty normal at our house. When the bell rang, everybody went directly to the table, and Dad stood behind his chair until every kid was in place. When he pulled out his chair, everybody sat down. Woe to the kid who wasn't there! He knew there'd be something coming. It was bad enough to get just a reprimand.

In our family, children were taught to join in the mealtime conversation and not to interrupt people. We were taught you don't discuss some things —murders, accidents or other horrors—at the table. We learned to talk about pleasant or instructive things, and we played games.

Our grandfather taught us all sorts of games. One was designed to make us remember things. The leader would start: "Here's a good fat hen, and about she goes." The kid to his right accepted this, turned to the next child, and said, "Here's a good fat hen, and about she goes."

That went all the way around, and the second time began: "Here are two ducks, a big fat hen, and about she goes." When that went around the next kid said, "Here's three plump partridges, two ducks, a good fat hen, and about she goes." That would circulate, with verses being added indefinitely. It not only taught us to remember, but to have fun to boot.

Another game we played was *gossip*. One wrote down a good long sentence and whispered it to the one next to him. He'd whisper it to the next child, who'd whisper it to the next, until it went clear on around yonder. When it came to the last kid, he'd write down what he heard and compare that to the original written message. Sometimes you wouldn't find even one word that matched. That game was fun, but it also involved serious teaching.

We were cccustomed to laughter, talk and good games at the dinner table. We had to pass the food clear around, and one of my brothers, who sat about halfway down, declared if he ever had a home of his own he'd never have to pass things. Almost the first thing he did when he married was build himself one of those Lazy Susan tables.

One dinner table episode that stands out in my mind violated all our rules about conversation, but showed just how understanding our father was. It involved our pet pig, a runt named Gee that Dad had let us raise by hand.

"You must feed it every day and take complete care of it," Dad warned. Eagerly we promised, and he gave us the little old runt. We nearly fed that pig to death. We not only fed him three times a day, but gave him plenty of variety, and we scrubbed and washed him till he didn't have a black hair on him! He was as pink as your hand.

Gee loved to be scratched. When he grew up he got so heavy that when he'd come bump up against us, he'd knock us over. Dad thought that was dangerous. One day he sent us all off to Grandpa's, and they butchered Gee. When we came home and couldn't find our pet, we cried ourselves to sleep.

The next morning they served us sausage for breakfast, and a horrible thought took shape in my mind. I don't know why, for I wasn't more than eight, but I connected that with Gee. When they put the sausage on my plate I began to sob, "Oh-h-h-h, it's Gee!"

Immediately everybody got to crying. You never heard anything like the commotion in all your life. When Dad looked around the table, tears rolled out of his eyes too. He called the cook to come take all that sausage away. He didn't make us eat that meat.

So our lives went on, sometimes happy and sometimes not. Those years, I ranged all over our plantation, seeing and doing and learning all I could. I had more curiosity than a cat and always wanted to do whatever I saw anybody else do. Because I was Marse Doc's daughter, the hands generally let me try what I pleased.

That's how, when I was eleven, I found myself in the cabinet shop learning to use the turning lathe. I made myself a croquet set with mallets and all, and formed the wickets with wire so strong it had to be heated before I could bend it.

As I made my last wicket, I somehow bent the end of the wire and had to cut it off. I heated it in the forge, put it on the anvil, and cut it off. Then the wire fell to the floor, and I stepped on it.

Did I dance around! I was barefooted, and I sailed around that shop till the blacksmith finally caught me and pulled the metal loose. I had the scar for the longest time.

Dad's drinking had become a steady habit by now, but he tried to be a good father. He was a born teacher who seldom missed a chance to teach us children something. For instance: once there was a lunar rainbow and Dad woke up every last kid, even our three-year-old, to see that phenomenon.

Another time there was a meteor shower. I can shut my eyes right now and see those stars, so brilliant they illuminated the sky as they fell; and I remember Dad once woke us all up to see the aurora borealis. That was wonderful!

We loved our father dearly and felt so close to him when he gave us such memory-making times, but we were growing up, getting to know Dad and to understand him better. Even I, who loved him so, no longer could pretend his steady drinking did him no harm.

For more than five years, day and night, he drank. I came to understand the unhappiness in our home, and to hate it. Whatever was to become of Dad?

The answer, as answers often do, arrived abruptly.

I Remember, I Remember

Dad's father and Mama's father got my father cornered one day and talked to him very earnestly until at last, heavy-hearted, he agreed to their urgings.

Dad must take himself in hand, our grandfathers said. He must straighten up and marry a good woman who'd come and raise those children.

3.
Mother

DAD MET Miss Annis Cushing through some of his friends. She was a settled woman of about thirty-five, still happy and young looking. I liked her light, soft voice and the very pretty way her hair curled around her face.

Miss Annis may have found it difficult to decide whether or not to marry my father, who by now possessed quite a mixture of good and bad traits, but this gentle, kind-hearted woman must have understood Dad. Evidently she cared for this hard-working, hard-drinking man, so burdened with sadness and the weight of heavy family and professional obligations.

If Dad knew hardship, however, so did Miss Cushing. Like other women of her time and place, she sacrificed unstintingly during the war. We can scarcely comprehend what those women did—and did without—during the long, terrible war years. Like the others, Miss Annis managed her family acreage, tended to the farmhands and livestock, ran the household, rolled bandages for the hospitals, and sewed uniforms and battle flags for the boys in gray. She could manage things; she had a streak of steel in her.

"I have no heart to offer you, because my heart is buried with Mary," Dad told Miss Cushing. "But if you'll marry me and help raise these children I'll give you a good home and make you a faithful husband."

She accepted him. I often told her, in later years, the only reason I suspected she didn't have good sense was that she took Dad on those terms!

I was twelve when Dad married Miss Annis, and I remember their wedding in a funny way.

We all went to Grandpa Glenn's house, for he was to perform the wedding ceremony. We children were very excited. Each of us harbored his own feelings about the marriage—some glad and some sad. The older kids remembered Mama too well not to have mixed feelings when Dad remarried, but the little boys and I felt just plain happy.

Despite all the excitement, I somehow fell asleep. Dad had gone to fetch Miss Cushing, and while we waited for what seemed forever, I just dropped off. When I woke up, the ceremony was over. I hadn't seen a bit of it!

Dismayed, I begged Dad and our new stepmother to go through the wedding again. They roared wih laughter, but wouldn't do it. They both looked so happy, however, that I swallowed my disappointment.

When it came time to take our new stepmother home, I started to crawl into the buggy beside Dad, where I always sat. He turned to me. "You sit next to Minnie, yonder," he suggested.

Quick as a flash, two soft arms went around me. "No, she comes right in here," my stepmother said, and pulled me in between them. The ride home felt wonderful.

That night, gathered around the fire for evening prayers, the family circle felt strange and somehow new, but it felt good, too. I turned to Dad's new wife.

"What name must I call you?" I asked her.

"I don't care what you call me, just so you love me," she answered softly.

I thought for a moment. "Well, I couldn't call you *Mama* because that was my own mama's name. How would *Mother* do?"

"I think *Mother* would do just fine," she said with a beautiful smile.

That night I knew I would love Mother. I always did, and she loved me. She was a wonderful Christian woman, very affectionate, and prepared to take on all of us children who'd let her. My oldest brother and sister never did accept Mother much, but she took over the rest of us and did the best she could.

Mother and I became great friends, and I always thought of her as being another girl. When my friends and I would exchange confidences and say, "Don't tell *anybody*," I'd always promise, "No, I won't tell *anybody!*," yet it never occurred to me to exclude Mother.

31

We enjoyed one another, and I loved her. Oh, how I loved her! If there's any place in heaven that's higher than any other, it ought to be reserved for good stepmothers.

Our home began to improve. With Mother there, life quickly became better regulated and more normal. Dad's drinking was about the only thing that didn't change.

Mother accepted that habit in silence, and put up with it. She was awfully patient with Dad. I can't remember ever hearing her complain, and she didn't let his drinking become an issue between them.

Then, when I was fifteen, I remember a particular court week in Conyers. The circuit judge came periodically to conduct court at the county seat, and social and business activities increased. Dad drank steadily throughout the week. One evening sitting before the fire, when Dad asked Mother to hand him his bottle, she seemed to gather up her courage.

"I wish you wouldn't take any more," she said quietly.

Dad shot her a look. "You talk like you thought I was drunk," he said.

Mother's sweet, steady gaze caught his eyes and held them. "I haven't seen you sober in a week," she told him.

Suddenly Dad reached for the quart bottle and dashed it into the open fireplace. Flames spewed out of the grate as the liquor exploded. In the bright light my father's face

32

looked strange and fierce, with an expression I couldn't interpret.

Although the flames burned his face and singed his beard and eyebrows, Dad didn't move. He sat stony faced. proud and absolutely motionless until the hot fire subsided.

I caught my breath and held it through the long, impetuous moment. My heart raced, and I ached for my father with the poor, burned face he wouldn't turn aside from the whiskey fire.

But a moment later, my pain subsided as quickly as the fire had done, for Dad didn't refuse to let Mother tenderly bathe his face with Mother Bush's Burn Medicine.

After that night, Dad never took another drink.

4.
Growing Up

WHEN SISTER Minnie got married and moved away, Dad and Mother had a consultation. I was growing up too, they realized, and at thirteen it was time I quit running about. I just ran with the little boys out yonder, and had become a regular tomboy. They decided I ought to learn to cook.

"Choose any meal you want, but you must start cooking one meal a day until you learn how to do it right," Dad said. This caused some consternation among my two younger brothers and me, because we did everything together. What one did, the others did too.

Still, it never occurred to either of them that this should be any different. Since I had to come in and cook, of course they'd help.

We decided we wouldn't choose supper since we'd have to stop playing, and we didn't want to come in from the woods, or from playing ball, to cook. Our big dinner in the middle of the day would be simply too much. That left breakfast, so breakfast was what we chose.

We didn't mind getting up early. Soon we caught on to

things and discovered it wasn't too hard to fix our family's morning meal of bacon, sausage or fried ham, grits, eggs, and hot biscuits. I usually cooked the biscuits. Everybody took on over the way we cooked and praised us to the skies.

But then the new kind of wore off. People quit taking on over us quite so much, and we'd gotten to where we thought we cooked pretty well; so I went to our parents.

"Don't you think we make pretty good biscuits now?" I asked.

"Yes-s-s-s," they agreed.

"Don't you think we fry meat pretty well?"

"Yes, it's fine."

I decided to press home my advantage. "Well, don't you think you could let us off from cooking breakfast now?"

Dad and Mother smiled at one another. Then Dad turned to me and spoke decisively. "Yes. Now you're going to start cooking dinner!"

So we went to work and learned to cook dinner. Whatever I did, the little boys did too, and whatever they did, I did.

If the boys could cook as well as I ever did, I knew how to play ball, swim, and climb trees just as well as they. If we weren't playing baseball, we were on the river or in the woods. Baseball, swimming, boating—there was something to do every minute, and if we weren't doing those things we probably were climbing trees.

Our favorite game (only our parents didn't know it), was to find a small tree that wasn't too much trouble to cut down. One of us would shinny up that tree clear to the top, and the others would cut the tree down. The art came in getting out of the tree as it toppled. When the tree started over, you know, you had to roll down with it instead of landing underneath it and getting smashed. Lord knows how we lived to grow up, but none of us kids broke any bones!

About that time I discovered dancing. I got so I'd rather dance than eat. My brother, Dutch, played the violin, and there were so many of us kids at home that when a few neighbors came in we could have a dance any time we wanted to. Dutch would get out his fiddle, strike up "Turkey in the Straw" or some other fast tune, and away we'd go. We'd have cotillions at our house or at the neighbors' quicker than you could say "scat": four people to the set, with four, eight, twelve or more of us jigging around the parlor. I always loved to dance the quadrille.

We kids grew up with a wonderful balance between freedom and responsibility, it seems to me. Besides all the fun, and the lessons our governess taught us, there were all sorts of other things to learn. Nobody especially made you learn things—you just wanted to.

Certainly nobody told me I should learn to read a blueprint, but when my older brothers went into the construction business, I just naturally wanted to puzzle out those interesting-looking plans they carried around with them. I still had more curiosity than a cat!

My big brothers patiently told me whatever I wanted to know, even though they thought I had no earthly use for knowing it. Certainly nobody dreamed I'd ever use that information in a far-off place like Brazil, or that my knowledge of blueprints one day would help break up a spy ring!

One thing nobody ever taught me was how to deal with children. I just knew. I took care of them all my life. By the time I turned seven I was lining up my little brothers, the plantation children, and whatever other little friends came around, and teaching school. It wasn't play, either. I was dead serious about it, and I taught several little Negroes to read.

Nobody dreamed then, of course, that at seventeen I'd start my real teaching career, with thirty-five children in a one-room school house.

So the time raced by. Mother saw that I learned the domestic arts, and Dad saw to our lessons. Otherwise, they left us to ourselves, and we all pried into whatever interested us most. Mother's mother, who had made so many soldier's uniforms during the war, taught me to tailor clothes. She came to live with us, and between them, they made everybody's clothes, including all the boys'.

I loved running the new sewing machine, so I gladly did

every bit of the stitching for them. I expect we bought the first sewing machine in town. Anyhow, I got right good at sewing. I'd rather tailor a man's suit right now than fool with a woman's dress.

When I wasn't studying, teaching, playing, dancing, or learning to cook, sew, read blueprints or do carpentry, I was pestering Dad. It seemed like I really wanted to become a doctor.

Now Dad let us kids pretty much alone in one way. He taught us early that we must make our own decisions and stick to them. He trained us up to be independent, and he taught us *how* to make decisions.

"Decide what is right," he said. "Strip down all the if's, and's and but's. Then act on the basic right." Consequently we learned very early to do the right thing without having to consult adults too often for advice. Maybe that's why I felt so hurt when I saw Dad was going to forbid me to study medicine.

I begged him, but he absolutely wouldn't hear of it. He said I had no business listening to some of the things I'd have to hear in order to become a doctor. That was that, with no discussion; or so we both thought at the time.

One thing I did for fun was send off for a correspondence course in a new subject called shorthand. Why? Still curious as a cat, I reckon. Anything there was that was new to learn, it seemed like I wanted to know about it. I smuggled paper into church with me and practiced my short-hand. I taught myself to take any preacher's sermon as fast as he could give it.

Neither Dad nor I dreamed that I'd use shorthand some day to learn, of all things, medicine.

I grew up, never quite figuring out where play ended and work began. I was a funny kid, I reckon—a rag-bag mixture of responsibility and harum-scarum, high-spirited one minute and serious the next. There's a funny story that shows what I mean.

I was fourteen, and conducting a "revival" service down in the woods. All our friends were there, lined up in rows like in church, and we were all just as serious about it. It wasn't a game with us, either. It was a real revival, with a mourners' bench and everything.

Naturally, I preached. I don't remember the sermon, but I do remember how fiery I got, how I waved my arms and shouted at them to repent. Then I called them forward.

Suddenly one of my girl friends got up and stumbled forward. She was a big girl, fourteen or fifteen, and plenty old enough to know what she was doing. She had repented and was converted.

Honest and truly, it was a *real* conversion. Then and there she accepted Jesus Christ as her Lord and Saviour. She joined the church after that, and began a really good Christian life.

I was old enough to recognize that her experience was real. The whole thing scared us all to death. Preaching was one thing, I thought, but converting people is another.

That was my last revival. I quit.

Since I was into my teens, I knew I must figure out what to do with my life. If Dad wouldn't let me become a doctor, what would I do instead? It was a puzzle, for everything interested me.

"Make your own decisions," Dad would say, and I knew I must, but there seemed to be no real hurry. Life on the old Yellow River plantation was too busy and full for me to wonder much about the future.

The older we got, meanwhile, the more our world seemed to expand. I'd always enjoyed studying geography and history, and now it interested me that Dad had become interested in Florida.

When one of Dad's friends traveled down there and reported the land was fabulously good, my father helped him borrow the money to buy 10,000 choice acres, including the present location of the city of Orlando.

Dad signed his friend's note, of course, for Mr. Grayson was an honorable man and good as gold; but when the time came to pay the note, Dad's friend couldn't pay it.

That's why, when I was fifteen, we sold our beautiful home place—just like that, overnight, it belonged to somebody else.

There was no help for it, of course. Dad naturally intended to stand behind his friend's security, and make the loan good.

5.
Adventures

OUR HOME WAS gone, so Dad's friend wrote us that we must come on down to Florida, where they'd share and share alike. I was curious about the place since Grandpa Glenn had gone to St. Augustine in 1823 as the first Methodist missionary ever assigned there.

My grandfather, a very methodical man, kept meticulous records in Florida of all the contributions made, who made them, and how much they were. I still have his old ledger.

He landed in Florida before the United States issued postage stamps. In those days you paid for your letters when you received them. Letters were written, folded, addressed, sealed with wax, and paid for on arrival. Grandfather's ledger even records how much he paid to receive his mail.

I thought about Grandfather Glenn's tales of Florida as Dad, Mother, the two little boys and I set out for that exotic place. It was the first real journey we kids ever had made—about 425 miles over today's roads, but much longer in those days.

We traveled to Jacksonville by train, then caught a steamer up the St. Johns River to Sanford. At Sanford, we took another train for Orlando. About halfway there, somewhere in the pine woods (I don't think they'd ever done any grading, but simply laid the rails down), the tracks simply spread apart and the little old engine just sat down in the sand.

What a fix! I haven't the least idea how they communicated, but somehow the railroad sent another engine up from the Orlando end of the line, and they picked us up in a freight car. Instead of arriving in Orlando at supper time, we fetched in at two in the morning.

If the train incident hadn't dampened our sense of adventure, our first view of Orlando the next morning should have. There was absolutely nothing there, except a great big weather-boarded building they called the hotel, and a few little skimped-up-and-down houses where people had taken lots and thrown up shacks to secure homesteads.

We kids scarcely were daunted, though our parents may have been. Early that morning, my two little brothers found a playmate and went fishing. My youngest brother never cared to fish, but he tagged along with the others. While they fished, he sat down on a nearby log to watch —and the log got up and walked off with him!

44

None of us ever had seen an alligator before. You should have seen those boys run! They returned to the hotel in double-quick time.

Our Florida adventure had lasted only three or four days when I overheard my father talking to his friend, Mr. Grayson. Mr. Grayson handed Dad a deed to half of the 10,000 acres of land, saying, "Dr. Glenn, you're obliged to make a comeback here. There's not a doctor this side of Jacksonville, and only one there. You'll make a living here without trying."

"Grayson," Dad replied, "I don't blame you for any of this. I believe you're an honest man, but I wouldn't live here if you gave me the whole 10,000 acres. I'm going back to God's country!"

Dad took the deed and tore it up. If he'd kept it, no telling what might have happened. We stayed in Florida a few days longer, then came back home to Georgia, where Dad started over in Conyers.

Our parents rented a house in town, and we kids started to school for the first time. School felt brand-new to us, and we liked it. In order to pay my way, I offered to assist with the younger pupils, and I liked that too. I'd had plenty of experience teaching, even before we moved to Conyers.

I found myself just as enthusiastic about living in town as I was about any other new thing to do. Losing our home,

45

moving to Florida, then returning to Georgia and moving to town—these events happened one behind the other, and so fast, I hardly could keep up. Life seemed very exciting.

Soon I passed another milestone, too, when I joined the Conyers Methodist Church. I was sixteen then and it just seemed time to take the step. Because it seemed natural and right, I did it.

It seems to me that the years unfolded like a long scenic postcard with myriad, interesting views.

My interest in medicine continued to be strong as I grew up. There was no arguing with Dad about it, however. He refused to let me become a doctor, and that was that. I knew I'd better think instead about what I *could* do, for it was time to begin supporting myself.

Accordingly, I took public examinations and became licensed to teach. I was just seventeen when the school board assigned me to teach in a one-room school house about twelve miles outside Conyers. There were thirty-five pupils, and some of the boys were bigger than I. I was hired to teach first grade through higher analytical arithmetic.

On the hot morning in September, 1873 when I opened my first school, the entire board of directors arrived to back me up. Beyond the open door we could see a day that shone as brightly as a new penny, all late-summer dazzle. Inside the dim, crowded room, the trustees stood about, surveying the children. Their chairman stepped forward.

"Miss Glenn," he proclaimed, "If these children don't

behave themselves and you can't manage to control them, just call us. We'll come help you out."

I hardly knew what to say, I was so astonished, but I knew I must reply.

"Gentlemen," I said firmly, "If ever I call you to come, it will be to accept my resignation. If I can't control these children myself, I'll resign."

I never doubted that I could handle the children, but sometimes their parents, surveying my blonde hair, green eyes and youthful face, looked dubious. That first morning, as I played with my children in the school yard, a man drove up with his small boy and girl and called me over to speak to him.

"Miss Glenn, I want you to understand that I don't allow anybody to whip my children," he began. I stood tall, looked him straight in the eye, and spoke with all the authority I could muster.

"Well, you'd better put them in the buggy and take them on, then," I told him calmly. "If they stay here, I'll whip them if they need it."

"I tell you, I don't allow *anybody* to whip my children," he said again.

"Take them on, then," I responded.

We exchanged long, searching looks, until at last he decided. "Well, I'll have to leave them."

Actually, I never had to whip those children or any others during my fifty years of teaching. I taught my kids that a look between me and them was all that was necessary, and discipline never was a problem.

"When I *look* at you," I told them, "you know what I mean." And they did.

My teaching career took me away from my parents' home for the first time in my life, to board with the Sims family. I opened our school at eight every morning, took dinner at noon, then worked until five in the afternoon. I'd go home to the Simses, where I tried to fit in like one of the family. I liked them and they liked me.

I taught the younger Sims children, but the two oldest boys were sent to school in Smyrna because they had a man teacher there. One night at supper the oldest boy mentioned that nobody, including the teacher, had been able to solve a certain arithmetic problem that day.

"*We* didn't have any trouble with it," said Simp, his younger brother who went to school with me.

Everybody turned and looked at me, but that's all that was said. Directly after supper I showed the older boys how to work the problem. They simply didn't understand the proposition. It was a rather long and complicated proposition, but when I helped them understand it they got the whole thing right off. Mr. Sims decided he'd made a mistake not to have those boys come to school with me. From then on, he had them study with me each night.

When I received my annual salary of seven hundred and

fifty dollars at the end of that year, I went to Mr. Sims to settle up my board. "You don't owe me one thing," he said.

"All right, I'll take it up with Mrs. Sims," I told him.

Mr. Sims, though he was married to her, still called his wife, "Miss Anne Prater."

"It's up to you and Miss Anne Prater," he told me, "and you can do what you please." But when I went to Mrs. Sims, she wouldn't listen.

"Why Miss Lonie," she protested, "I'd just as soon think about taking board from my little kitty!"

They wouldn't let me pay one penny. Today, in Conyers, I still count the grandchildren of the Sims children among my good friends.

The teaching profession took me from one country school to another all over Rockdale County for nearly ten years, and the work suited me right down to the ground. I loved the children and enjoyed the challenge, and the days and weeks seemed to fly.

Then I was sent to Oxford, a little town close to the plantation where I grew up. Because Emory University had had its beginnings in the pretty little Oxford town, there always had been a lively Methodist community there.

At Oxford I became friends with a very good and deeply spiritual woman, Mrs. Callaway, a dedicated Methodist lay worker who changed the course of my life. It was Mrs. Callaway who suggested that I consider training myself for the mission field.

Foreign missions? The more I considered that intriguing idea, the more logical it seemed. As Dad had taught me to do, I considered the thing from all angles. It didn't take long to see that becoming a missionary would suit me fine.

Everything seemed to add up. Grandpa Glenn had been a missionary, of course. My parents and their parents had given me a strong religious background. My natural curiosity, I now saw, had allowed the Lord to outfit me with all sorts of odd skills that might be useful in a foreign land.

Mrs. Callaway's friend, Miss Maria Gibson, intended to open a training school for missionaries in Kansas City. Mrs. Callaway believed I'd do good work in the mission field, so she proposed to have the Methodist women sponsor my training.

Besides, there was another incentive; the new training school would teach not only Bible, but nursing as well. Here was the medical teaching I'd always wanted!

Since I was free, white and twenty-six, I told Mrs. Callaway I'd gladly train to become a missionary. Now I needed only to break the news to my parents, and I could hardly wait to tell them!

Imagine my surprise when I saw that Dad was adamantly opposed to the scheme.

"I'd rather see you dead!" he growled, and he refused to go into the subject.

"But Dad," I protested, "I'm doing exactly what you taught me to do. You're the one who always insisted that I make my own decisions and stick to them."

"More fool I" he said bitterly.

Dad had taught his lesson well. He forbade me to take missionary training, but he would not give his reasons. Therefore, since his position seemed unreasonable, I took his early advice and did exactly what seemed right. I enrolled in Scarritt Bible and Training Institute. I never did discuss with my father whether or not I should become a nurse. Why should I, I thought, when he seemed so unwilling to consider my vocation toward the mission field?

A real rift developed between my father and me, for the first time. Unhappy as the situaton made us, it nevertheless did nothing to change my mind. My father, after all, had taught me to follow my conscience, regardless of feelings.

To make matters worse, I received a letter from a supposed friend of mine, who had met my father and asked him about me.

"I know nothing about Layona," she quoted Dad as saying. "As far as I am concerned, she is dead."

6.
Missionary Training

DAD DIDN'T LIKE my decision to travel to Kansas City, Missouri, to matriculate at the new Scarritt Bible and Training Institute. "I'd just as soon you'd be dead as do that," he had told me, and I knew he meant it; but I went on anyway.

Mrs. Callaway took me to Atlanta to the train. She had written ahead to recommend me to her friend, Miss Maria Gibson, who was to direct the new school.

"Give Miss Maria a kiss for me," she called as the train pulled out of the station. I waved to Mrs. Callaway and promised to do just that.

Accordingly, when I met Miss Maria Gibson the very next morning in the Scarritt social hall, adjoining her bedroom, I reached over and kissed her. A very definite extension of her arm showed me I had made a mistake!

Miss Gibson was a very fine woman, I saw at once, but she had a certain reserve. She had run a private school for young ladies before taking over Scarritt, and she meant to impose the same rules she'd used to train those young schoolgirls on us women missionary trainees. At twenty-six, I was one of her youngest students, yet she didn't allow a one of us to go to town without a chaperone.

Well, that was 1892. Things are different now. The fact was, Scarritt Bible and Training Institute was the first school of its kind in the Southern Methodist Church. Its purpose was to prepare women for Christian work in all types of service, at home and in other lands. Up till then, any young woman who felt called to devote her life to the Lord's work in foreign lands was accepted and sent out without any training whatever. No matter what her work and responsibility in the field might be, she had to tackle it unprepared, and develop her own system and ability by experience in the field.

The Scarritt student body was small that first year. We had thirteen students and twenty-three teachers, and each teacher gave us written and oral examination!

We had a fascinating course of study. There was Bible instruction (of course) comparative religions, vocal and instrumental music, evidences of Christianity and allied subjects, and housekeeping and domestic service. Because the Methodist Church in the Orient needed nurses and doctors for women and children, Scarritt operated a very efficient small hospital with a competent medical staff and administrative personnel to provide such training.

All students were required to take the entire curriculum, but each of us majored in certain things. We undertook a tremendously heavy course, as you can see.

I decided to major in Bible study. Again, this was my decision, made without asking anyone else's advice. I recalled my friend's statement that my father had said, that so far as he was concerned, I was dead. When I wrote Mother, my stepmother, about what I'd heard, she didn't say aye, yes, or no.

"You know how your father is, so set in his ways," she wrote. "Just don't pay any attention to him." Always before then, I had written to Dad and Mother together. After that time, I wrote to Mother only.

I didn't have to ask Dad to know how he felt. I knew he opposed my studying medicine, or serving in the Orient. I found I could not disregard his wishes; so, although I enjoyed my medical courses and got everything out of them that I could, I decided to major in Bible.

Meanwhile, my new life at the new school was proving to be as interesting as anything I'd ever experienced. Part of this was because of Miss Maria (she pronounced it Mar-EYE-a) Gibson. I could not figure her out.

When I'd been at Scarritt only a few days, she sent for me. "Miss Glenn, I have to ask you not to *monopolize* the conversation at table," she said.

I was astonished. I was twenty-six and had taught school for nearly ten years. Naturally I took part in the table conversation. We had been trained as children to participate, and to know one did not interrupt, and that there were certain things one did not talk about at table.

"I wasn't conscious that I talk too much," I Miss Gibson. "I won't do it any more."

From then on my table conversation consisted of "No, thank you", and "Yes, please". Miss Gibson sent for me again.

"What's the matter now, Miss Gibson?"

"The way you're acting at the table," she scolded. "Everybody's talking about it!"

"Miss Gibson," I said, "if you'll tell me what you want me to do, I'll try my very best."

"All I want is for you to be your natural self," she said.

"That's what I thought I had been doing!"

I was genuinely puzzled. She meant her criticism kindly and I took it that way, but it became something of a task to take part in the conversation for just the right amount, neither too much nor too little, to suit Miss Maria!

To make matters worse, there was the dining hall procedure. We ate at big tables which seated eight, with the teachers sitting among the students. At the end of each week, the girls rotated from one table to another—all except me. I never was rotated! For some reason, I sat right in front of Maria Gibson for the whole two years. I reckon so she could keep her eye on me there.

Shortly after I arrived at Scarritt, Miss Gibson received a letter from our mutual friend, Mrs. Callaway, which she displayed at the breakfast table. Then she turned to me.

"Mrs. Callaway says she sent me a message by you, but you never delivered it," she reproached.

"What was that, Miss Gibson?"

"She said you were to give me a kiss."

"Why, I gave it to you the first day I came, Miss Gibson," I said. I wish you could have seen her face.

Miss Maria Gibson and I got along well enough, however. I liked my courses and my fellow students enormously. I very quickly decided the faculty was grand, and that Miss Holden, who taught me Bible, was one of the best teachers anywhere.

Unlike some of the other students, I had grown up reading the Bible and had heard it read at family prayers every day of my life. I considered myself fairly familiar with God's word—then I met Miss Holden. She made us conduct our own Bible study, and she had a wonderful method which made the Holy Bible became an indelible part of a student's life.

"Your rule for studying the Bible, whether you learn it by book, chapter, or verse, is to read it carefully three times," she told us.

"First read it just as you would a newspaper story, then read it very carefully a second time, taking note of the people, places and dates. The third time you read it, learn what those people and things did."

Thus we started at Genesis and worked our way straight through the Holy Bible. We learned every bit of it by our own independent study. I wouldn't take the world for Miss Holden's training.

This training undoubtedly was the most valuable thing I got during my two years at Scarritt. I have used Miss Holden's method of Bible study every day of my life, from 1892 until today, and it's still exciting.

Often I try to blot out all memory of the Bible, and read it as though it were my very first time. I just can't do it, because I grew up with those words.

I was raised up with the *King James Version of the Holy Bible,* and learned my ABC's from Mama's beautiful *King James* volumes. I still think it's the most beautiful English we have or ever will have, and it's so clear.

I still continue my personal adventure with God's word. I study it in a number of different ways. For example, I might study the characters of the Bible. This has led to some exciting discoveries.

I remember noting how, when God called Moses to go to Egypt to release his people, God told Moses, "*I am,*" (Exodus 3:14). *I am* is an unfinished statement, of course, but it was enough to let Moses know the eternal, existing God was with him. Moses accepted *I am.* Later Jesus came into the world to demonstrate God's character and show what He is.

Moses heard God say, "*I am,*" and Jesus, of course, completed the statement for us: ". . . *The bread of life.*"

Sometimes people ask me to name my favorite book of

the Bible. It's the Gospel according to St. John. If all of the Bible were lost but the book of John, there'd be enough to save the world. If all the book of John were lost but the third chapter, there still would be enough to save the world. And if all the third chapter except the sixteenth verse were lost, there *still* would be enough to save the world, for it says:

> *For God so loved the world, that he gave his only begotten Son, that whosoever believeth in him should not perish, but have everlasting life.*

I call John 3:16 the whole Gospel, captured in one sentence.

7.
Graduation

EACH WEEK at Scarritt, we girls took turns leading the prayer meeting. One of the girls who majored in nurse's training never had read or studied the Bible. We thought she was a regular heathen!

One night she came down just as prayer meeting began. She'd had a stretch of night duty, so she hadn't attended prayer meeting regularly. It happened that was the night her name turned up to lead the service.

"I'm not prepared," she told Miss Gibson in some alarm.

"No young lady should ever say she's not prepared for anything," Miss Gibson replied, and made her lead the meeting.

The poor flustered girl started reading a Bible passage that ends "... with the wiles of the devil" (Ephesians 6:11), but she read it wrong. Somehow she read "the *whales* of the devil." Then, as if that weren't bad enough, she got down to pray and she prayed for the Lord to protect us from those whales!

I thought we'd all die. It should have taught Miss Gibson

a lesson if it didn't teach anybody else. After that, the girl came to my room often and I helped her all I could. She went on to become a good Bible student and a good missionary.

Scarritt, of course, was a Bible and training school. The training meant nurse's training, and for this they used staff members from the medical school downtown. The doctors gave us the same lectures they gave the young male medical students, and I took down every word in shorthand.

Besides the lectures, we took a certain amount of training in the little Scarritt hospital. We Bible students took just theoretical training, with a few extra things such as the art of bandaging.

Since I'd wanted to become a doctor, this part of my course interested me very much. The lectures, for the most part, were excellent; however, I remember one doctor who had no more sense than a cat. He gave the same lecture over and over, the same old matter, until eventually the authorities heard of it.

I took all his lectures down in shorthand. One day they wanted to know about this doctor, so they asked for my shorthand book. After a secretary transcribed his lectures from my book, they dismissed that doctor from the staff.

The rest of our training was very valuable. I had gone to Scarritt for nurse's training just as much as anything else and when I finished my two-year course there, I received a diploma in nursing. I hadn't asked Dad's advice about the nurse's training. I doubt that he would have approved, but in any case we were not in communication with one another.

The first year hurried by. We worked so hard we could scarcely keep up with ourselves, and it was *interesting*. Then came summer. After that long, hard year, you can imagine how I longed to go home.

It would be nice to get away from Miss Maria Gibson's absurd rules for a few weeks, I thought. I longed to see Mother and the rest of the family. Yes, and though I didn't know how Dad would receive me, it would be good to go home and attempt to square things with him.

But I didn't go home. Because I couldn't afford to make the trip, I spent the summer at Scarritt. The other six members of my Bible class departed, however, full of comments about Miss Gibson's strict rules. Imagine my astonishment when none of them returned the following year. This gave me the high honor of becoming the first graduate of Scarritt's Bible Department, by default!

I didn't want to waste the summer. Charlie Scarritt spent the summer at school too, and he and I decided to do something about the huge stacks of donated books that had poured into the institution. Charlie knew something about library work, so we agreed we'd better get those volumes out of their packing boxes and onto the shelves.

All summer we sorted, separated and shelved books. We

cataloged them, listed them according to subjects and authors, and arranged them that way on the shelves. It was backbreaking work. Charlie and I were mighty glad to see the last of that big job.

Then school started again. I'll never forget the girl from Texas who was put in charge of the library. Charlie and I thought we'd put it in perfect condition for her, but Irene was an orderly soul. She took one look at our shelves, with big and little books together all higgledy-piggledy, and didn't like what she saw.

She went in there and swept the whole business out, and proceeded to arrange the books according to *size*. I could hardly believe my eyes. The system we'd worked all summer to create had been destroyed!

"Well, honey, I'll just have to put you in here and let you straighten it out again," Miss Gibson suggested.

"I'll go home first!" I swore.

Since I was the only student in the Bible Department who had stood the gaff, I decided to work extra hard my second year. There was plenty to learn, plenty to do, and I had no idea how the Lord might use me after graduation. I worked on, laboring toward I knew not what.

Graduation day came at last. How I had looked forward to it, and what a funny day it turned out to be!

That evening Miss Holden, who had become my dear friend, asked me before the cermonies to arrange her hair

Then Miss Gibson saw Miss Holden's hair, and wanted me to fix hers the same way.

Well, you couldn't do a thing with Miss Gibson's hair the way you could Miss Holden's. I worked and worked on that woman's hair, all the time conscious that time was getting away. I hadn't even thought about getting myself ready for my graduation exercises. When Miss Gibson was satisfied at last, I rushed to my room and flung on my clothes, then raced to the streetcar that took us to Central Methodist Church for the ceremonies.

In the brightly lighted car, somebody reached over and touched my skirt. "Miss Glenn, you've got your dress on wrong side out!" she exclaimed. When I got to church I had to rush downstairs, take off my dress and put it on again right side out.

At last I was ready to enjoy my graduation. Now I could listen to the bishop's words as he presided, and enjoy the music and songs. Then it was time for me to read my valedictory speech and receive my diploma.

It was May, 1894. I was twenty-eight, and ready to begin my career in foreign missions. That night, thinking of the marvelous training I'd received at Scarritt, I felt my heart fill to the brim with gratitude. The only thing I wouldn't miss about the place, I told myself honestly, was Miss Maria Gibson. Much as I admired her, I would be glad to be rid of Miss Gibson!

There's a funny little footnote to our relationship. Years

after I graduated from Scarritt, I returned to an alumnae meeting. I was seated at the head table, prepared to speak on foreign missions, when I was asked to offer a toast to Miss Gibson. The idea filled me with dismay.

I thought I absolutely could not do it. I could not think of one thing to say. Even when they introduced me and I got to my feet, I had not thought of a toast to propose. I stood there a minute and prayed the hardest prayer I ever did pray; then I began to speak.

"Miss Gibson, you started a training school, and you also were in training. I *know* we tried your soul, because I know how you tried ours!

"The fact is, we never realized what you meant and what you had to do until we got out on the mission field where we had to take your place, and do the work you are doing here. The farther we got from you, Miss Gibson, the better we loved you!"

The crowd seemed to be convulsed. They cheered and laughed, and cheered and laughed, and they didn't stop. When they kept going that way, I commenced to get alarmed. "You fool, what *did* you say?" I asked myself.

I thought I'd better try to set things to rights, so I waved them down and got to my feet again.

"Some things are so great we have to get far enough away from them to get the perspective," I said. "When we start at the foot of the great Rocky Mountains, the only thing that impresses us is the roughness and difficulty of the footwork. We have to get far enough away to get a perspective to see the beauty of the mountain with snow on top.

"Miss Maria Gibson, that's the way we had to get far enough away from you, to get the perspective."

I guessed I'd saved the situation. Miss Gibson seemed to like the toast, and the crowd continued to cheer and laugh. Most important, I thought, I hadn't said one word that was not absolutely true!

8.
My Departure

How would it be to go home? I wondered. I had not written one line to Dad in two years. That hurt me, and I knew it hurt him just as badly.

As I packed to return home, and as I thought about my first missionary assignment, I wondered also how Dad might receive me. I just didn't know.

When I reached Conyers, Dad was on the platform to meet me. We simply took up where we had left off. Neither said a word about all that had happend. We each knew one another's stubbornness, understood it and forgave it. So Dad took me home, and it was all right.

About three weeks after I was graduated from Scarritt, in May, 1894, the North Georgia meeting was held in Atlanta, and my application was presented there for missionary work. My friend Mrs. Callaway was our district leader of the Women's Missionary Society, and I felt as pleased for her as I did for myself when the board accepted me as a missionary candidate and appointed me to Brazil.

This was not a routine appointment. Because of the dreaded yellow fever, Brazil was considered a dangerous assignment. The mission board didn't send you there, but asked if you'd be willing to go. I reckon they figured if you volunteered and died it would be suicide, whereas if they sent you and you died, it would be murder!

Seriously, I didn't mind the idea of Brazil at all. My father would not consent to my going to the Orient, but he reluctantly agreed to allow me to go to Latin America. The thought of yellow fever didn't scare me. I'd never seen it. Besides, I was a strong, healthy girl and thought I knew quite a bit about medicine.

"I'll go," I told the Mission Board. "I'm not worried about yellow fever. Anyhow, I'm not accustomed to taking anything that doesn't belong to me, so I won't take it!"

My father was surprisingly agreeable to the appointment. The whole time I was at Scarritt he had been like a stranger to me. Now I was home, briefly, and he'd changed around and made up his mind to accept my decision and let me go. Dad knew me well enough to know he wanted to get that thing, that strangeness we'd let grow up between us, straightened out before I left.

He and Mother pitched in and did everything in the world to help me. I had been appointed to Brazil for five years. Goodness, I'd need everything under the sun!

Mother immediately started stitching a new wardrobe

which she hoped would carry me through five years of we-didn't-know-what. She was a dandy seamstress, and she worked night and day for three weeks; of course I helped, too.

Dad also did everything he possibly could to help. He took over the packing. He fitted the books I so carefully selected—the Bible, my commentaries and my reference books—into a large wooden crate, and nailed the lid down securely.

He also fixed up a lot of medical supplies for me. He included drugs I wouldn't be able to get down there, and things like camphor, that he knew I ought to have.

Dr. Logan, the ear, nose and throat man from Scarritt, also was very nice to me. At school he had let me come into his office and watch him treat people, and he'd explain to me what he was doing and why. He sent me a surgical kit for ear, nose and throat treatment. It was a wonderful gift, and I have some of those things yet.

"You use these," he wrote. "You know how, and you can use them just as well as I can."

The days sped by. I had only two months between graduation and my sailing date, and we filled each day to the brim. As the time to go rushed toward me, Dad and Mother became more and more loving and concerned, and I became more eager for the adventure ahead.

The Methodist Church had been working in Brazil about

fifteen years, I knew. Miss Martha Hite Watts had been our first missionary there, and I was to travel to Brazil with her and help her establish Methodist schools in that predominately Roman Catholic country. There were several other Methodist missionaries in Brazil besides Miss Watts by the time they appointed me, but it still was considered quite a challenge. It was such new work.

When people ask if I felt intimidated by the size of the job, I say that's what I trained for—nor was I apprehensive. It was, after all, the thing I'd worked so hard to fit myself for, but Dad was horrified!

At last I was packed and ready. I was to leave the next morning at six. That night Dad and I sat together on the front veranda. He got up and walked into the yard, and looked up at the stars. They were bright as could be.

Pointing to the Big Dipper up yonder, Dad instructed me in his best school teacher voice: "Theoretically, I know that the stars will not appear in the southern hemisphere, where you are going, as they do up here. But knowing a thing theoretically and seeing it yourself, or hearing it from someone who has seen it, are two different things. When you get down there I want you to write me and tell me exactly how these stars appear from down there."

It was right funny and sweet. Of course I saw straight through Dad's little stratagem.

"All right, Dad," I promised, loving him very much. "I will write. I'll let you know."

I wrote Dad from every stopping place, Baltimore, New York and all the rest. As long as I lived in Brazil and my father was alive, no steamer ever arrived there without a letter to me from Dad.

9.
Journey to Brazil

DAD AND MOTHER took me to Atlanta, where I was to begin my journey to Brazil. They shipped my things through to New York, and I boarded the train for Washington, D. C., where I was to meet my distinguished traveling companion, Miss Martha Hite Watts.

I found Miss Watts surrounded by the largest pile of luggage you ever did see. Boxes, trunks and valises seemed to stretch out forever, and she was trying to keep track of it all. When she spied me, she took one look at the one small handbag I carried and asked in real horror, "Is that *all* you're taking to Brazil?"

When Miss Watts and I entrained for New York City to begin our long steamship journey, I found myself filled with anticipation. This was the woman who had pioneered on behalf of the Methodist Church in Brazil. Singlehandedly, she started schools, churches and missions. Her efforts had been remarkably successful.

One by one other men and women had followed her, and now I was to be one of them. What would be my part in the great Brazilian effort? How could I help carry out the formidable projects Miss Watts had begun?

When we boarded the steamer in New York for our twenty-three-day trip to Rio de Janeiro, my respect for my doughty little fellow traveler increased a thousandfold. Miss Watts, when she first embarked for Brazil fifteen years earlier, had had to journey to London and thence to South America. Now she congratulated us on our luck; the Lamport and Holt steamship line could get us to Brazil in just over three weeks, and we could bypass London!

I got so seasick, I could only moan. Strong, healthy, unaccustomed to illness, I nevertheless had fallen prey to what I felt sure must be the worst malady known to man —seasickness.

My mal de mer, despite my determination, simply would not yield to willpower. I couldn't keep a thing on my stomach. For fifteen days everything I ate came up. When I yielded to the doctor's concern and heeded the Biblical injunction to "use a little wine for thy stomach's sake" (1 Timothy 5:23), even that came back up.

Still, sick as I was for those fifteen days, I could not feel really discouraged, nor did I regret my decision. I wasn't at all sorry I'd chosen Brazil, though like Mark Twain I *was* afraid I wouldn't die!

At Bahia, Miss Watts and I were supposed to put ashore to visit a missionary family. It seemed out of the question for me, but as land came in sight I began to revive, and I was determined to accompany Miss Watts.

There was no place to dock, and the steamer had to lie way out in the bay. Those going ashore had to get into small boats which the crew rowed toward land. The doctor strongly advised me not to go—I had been so sick he was sure I'd die before we reached Rio—but I went.

Don't ask me how, I just went. I was determined to put my feet on land that day. The missionary couple met Miss Watts and me and took us to their home for lunch. For one time in this life I filled up! They must have been astonished to see me, thin, pale and peaked as I was, eating like a farmhand. I didn't bother explaining about my illness, but simply proceeded to eat everything in sight, especially the chicken pie, a favorite of mine.

After I touched land and ate all that good food, I never was seasick another minute. The trip from Bahia to Rio was beautiful.

We arrived at Rio de Janeiro on August 26, 1894, four days before the state of siege ended and the new republic was secured.

It was late in the day, a Sunday. There were no docks at Rio then, and our vessel had to anchor far out in the bay. No one was allowed to come aboard for us, so we had to lie at anchor all night and wait for permission to land on Monday.

I felt impatient, of course, that we could not land. What a unique experience to stand on deck out there in the water, watching the sudden tropical darkness fall upon us. The lights came on, one by one, twinkling around the bay —on the Rio side, up on the hillsides, and on the other side along the Nictheroy shore.

Beside us, lights came on in the other silent vessels that crowded the bay, and high above, the stars glittered brightly in what I suddenly realized was a soft, early spring night!

That first breathtaking view of Rio de Janeiro will remain with me as long as I live. I've often wished I could paint it. I wish I could reproduce for you, side by side, the Guanabara Bay of that night, and the same view today.

Then, lamplighters had to run along every street and light each individual lamp. Today, Rio, like any other modern city, blazes with electric illumination. That night Sugar Loaf and Corcovado mountains loomed huge and silent against the blackness. Tonight they shine out of the gloom in a blaze of glory, proud sentinels guarding one of the world's most majestic cities.

That night in August, 1894, I knew at once I would love the indescribable grace and beauty of Brazil, but I did not dream how deep that love could go, and how long it would last.

10.
I Begin My Mission

I HAD BEEN appointed to Petrópolis, a handsome suburb high in the mountains beyond Rio de Janeiro, where Miss Watts and I planned to open a new Methodist school. We arrived before the property transfer took place, however, so it became necessary to make interim plans.

While she went on to Juiz de Fora to inspect our Colegio Mineiros, I stayed in Rio for ten days with the very hospitable Reverend and Mrs. H. C. Tucker, who lived next door to the Methodist Church on Largo do Cattete.

Everything I saw in Rio those days reinforced my first impressions of its grandeur. Here were broad avenues lined with stately royal palm trees, impressive modern buildings, and elegantly dressed citizens gracing one of the world's most enchanting cities.

Here also, amid lush trees and bougainvillea blossoms, an ineffably balmy seaside climate, and startling views of mysterious mountains which arose from the sea, you could see, as you can in all large cities, a full measure of the dreadful human misery, poverty and disease which looks so terribly out of place against the wonder of God's creation.

Surely, I thought, no other place on earth can be more beautiful than this, yet never before have I seen so many desperately deprived people, especially the children. Born of every race and nationality under the sun, and every mixture of these, Brazilian children run the full range of human beauty, and all seem to possess engaging charm. I loved them at once.

At that time, Mrs. Tucker served as directress of the Colegio Americano Fluminense, which Miss Watts had established and which was housed in the Cattete Chapel and a couple of rooms in the Tucker home. The Tuckers urged Miss Watts to let me stay there to direct the school, and Mrs. Tucker promised to help me until I learned the language and could assume the responsibility alone.

In those days, missionary appointments were made in the United States, often quite arbitrarily, and nobody dared change anything about them. Since I had been appointed to help Miss Watts establish the Colegio Americano in Petrópolis, she said she couldn't change that, even though we would not be able to begin the work for some months.

Instead, Miss Watts and I went to a school in Piracicaba while we awaited the transfer of the Petrópolis property. I was eager to see the town, whose name means "place where the fishes stop." Miss Watts had established one of our oldest Methodist schools there fifteen years earlier, and I was curious to see how this institution, thriving with one hundred pupils, was run.

Before we departed from the Tucker home in Rio, Miss Watts decided we'd stop off at Taubaté to visit the family of the Reverend J. L. Kennedy, president of the Methodist school there. Accordingly, she sent him a telegram to advise that our train would arrive at six that evening. As we left Rio, I little dreamed of the dramatic advenure that awaited me at Taubaté.

Our train, detained for some reason, arrived five hours late. When we piled out into the deep night, laden with luggage, we found the tiny station deserted except for the station master and one late hanger-on. It was an intimidating scene. The station, lit with only one smoky hanging lantern, was plunged in murky darkness when the train pulled out.

Worse, when Miss Watts inquired about Mr. Kennedy, she learned he had not come to the depot that night.

What must we do? We decided to leave our luggage at the station and let the hanger-on show us the way to Brother Kennedy's house.

There were no street lights. The streets were unpaved and mud sloshed shoe-mouth deep. Somehow we managed to slip and slide along behind the questionable-looking man, who led us an interminable distance through dark, silent streets before he stopped outside a house he identified as the Kennedys'.

"Oh! *de casa!*" Miss Watts called loudly, clapping her hands smartly.

That was the first time I heard the call, "You of the house!" Eventually an upstairs window opened and a head appeared, and then I learned a second phrase of Portuguese. *"Quiem é?"* (Who is it?)

The door opened, and our explanations flew thick and fast. No telegram had been delivered! Worse, the Taubaté school was in process of being moved to São Paulo. Everything had been loaded into freight cars except what the family needed that night, and the family with its remaining household goods would be loaded on the *mixto* (mixed trains) early the next morning.

It must have been two o'clock before *café* had been served, the urgent "first talk" over, and we all got to bed. I learned the next morning that although Wallace, her baby, was only three weeks old, Mrs. Kennedy gave her bed to Miss Watts and me and put a mattress on the floor for herself and the baby.

As we sipped our morning *café*, the men came to take the rest of the furniture to the station. Then Mrs. Kennedy, after seeing that everyone else was served, went to look after the baby—and could not find him!

We searched, feeling first somewhat foolish, then alarmed. We discovered the movers, thinking the tiny bundle on the pallet was a pillow, had rolled Wallace up with the bedclothes, tied up the bundle and put it on the cart.

We opened the bundle feverishly, to find baby Wallace all but suffocated. His face had begun to turn blue. Poor Mrs. Kennedy, thinking her baby was dead, burst into tears and clasped him to her bosom.

My nurse's training made me know the urgent necessity for attempting artificial respiration. I snatched the baby from her and went to work on him. Seeing my intention, Brother Kennedy restrained his distraught wife, so I could apply first aid. After a few terrible moments, little Wallace began to breath normally. When he gave a lusty cry, I handed him to his mother, who then could do much more for him than I.

The excitement was over, except for arrival of the telegram informing the Kennedys of our coming. Had we not invaded their home that night, I reflected, the accident likely never would have happened; but since it did, my hospital training already had justified itself.

We accompanied the Kennedy family to São Paulo, then continued to Piracicaba, arriving on September seventh, a Friday. There it was decided that I would be assigned to the big Piracicabo school while we waited to open the new one in Petrópolis.

Believe it or not, the following Monday I found myself in charge of the kitchen, where I was to cater for the household of one hundred people!

There was no time for dismay. Not only must I supervise the dining room and kitchen, but I must do the marketing, plan the meals, and direct the work of the cook and half a dozen girls who did domestic work to pay their tuition.

Imagine! Not only did I know no Portuguese, but I'd never thought of such a thing as buying a vegetable. At home, if we wanted cabbage we went out and cut it; if we wanted turnip greens, we went out and picked them. Here, I'd have to buy these things. I just had to do it! I reckon I spent a whole lot of money I ought not to, but I went right out and commenced doing the buying.

Obviously, I needed to learn Portuguese right away. During my off hours I devoted myself feverishly to the study of the language. Soon I became somewhat disgusted with the other missionaries, who hesitated, and sometimes downright refused, to speak the language or to use it in prayer. I was determined to talk, and to use every word I learned.

When I could not express a complete thought in Portuguese I filled in the gaps with English. Sometimes the results were amusing, sometimes harrowing in the extreme for my poor listeners.

"Miss Glenn, for heaven's sake keep your mouth closed until you learn Portuguese," one teacher advised me.

Had I followed her advice, my mouth still would be shut. However, I paid no attention to her, but continued to talk to all who would listen. If they laughed at my mistakes I asked them to explain, so I could laugh too. The Brazilians enjoyed my efforts, appreciated them, and were unfailingly tactful and helpful with me.

The school Miss Watts had founded at Piracicabo fairly inspired me to learn all I could. The large, bustling institution, so hard to shop and cook for because of its size, had started, Miss Watts said, with just one pupil. Now it was fairly bursting at the seams. Miss Watts often told me how much she valued my help there, and before we'd worked together six months she called me the best aide she'd ever had.

I drove myself to learn Portuguese. One way, I decided, would be to practice taking the Sunday sermons in shorthand. At church someone always was kind enough to find the Bible selection for me, and the hymns. I'd try to follow as the Lesson was read, and the familiar Methodist hymns sung, in my unfamiliar but beautiful new language.

Portuguese is a highly phonetic tongue, so I found I could take the sermons in shorthand quite easily. One Sunday in November, Brother Dickey, our presiding elder, arrived to lead the Quarterly Conference, and to preach. That night he took dinner with us at the college.

"How much of my sermon did you understand this morning?" he teased me.

"Enough to take down the outline," I answered quite seriously. Brother Dickey looked skeptical. When I whipped out my shorthand pad and showed him the sermon outline I had made as he preached, the good man looked quite taken aback.

"Either I anglicise my Portuguese unforgivably," he said in some astonishment, "or you're a prodigy at learning the language."

"You must anglicise, then," I joshed him. "There's really no miracle about it, Brother Dickey, just the miracle of hard work and the determination to speak Portuguese. I try not to think in English. I go to sleep at night telling myself a story in Portuguese. I mean to speak to these people in their language very soon."

And I did.

11.
School Ma'am Again

I NEVER ALLOWED myself to get homesick. If I got homesick, I was coming home. I went to Brazil with the understanding that I would stay five years, and I never allowed myself to think anything else.

It was *my* will to go to Brazil and follow God's will. Right away I discovered He had pretty much the same plan for me here that he'd had back in Georgia. I was to work with children.

That spurred me on with my language studies. Many of the missionaries who had arrived three or four years earlier still couldn't say a prayer in Portuguese, I noticed. I decided that would not do, not for me.

One day as I sat watching my children at play, a little English-speaking girl queried me, "Miss Glenn, can you say the Lord's Prayer in Portuguese?"

"No, not yet."

"Miss Glenn don't know the Lord's Prayer in Portuguese," she teased, giggling mischievously.

One of the other little girls immediately came up and put her arm around my shoulder.

"Don't you worry, Miss Glenn," she comforted me, "I think the Lord understands English!"

I think the good Lord must have understood my real need to translate my English to some sort of Portuguese those kids could understand, too. I must get right to work trying to train them, for it seemed to me they needed to develop some sense of responsibility.

Often there was a problem about their telling the truth, too. Gradually I made my kitchen helpers understand that they were expected to accept their little responsibilities, and that they *must* tell the truth. When they told the truth, I emphasized, their punishment, if any, always would be meted out fairly and kindly.

One of the girls' regular tasks was that of closing up the kitchen and dining rooms at night. The school directress, Miss Alice Moore, told me I must always check their work and make sure the doors and windows were secure before I went to bed.

That troubled me a little. I knew the girls expected me to check on them, but I considered that bad training. One day I called my little group together and told them I would not check on their work any more. We talked about honesty and dependability, and our Christian responsibility to one another, until I was satisfied that we understood one another perfectly.

"I'll never spy on you girls again," I told them. "You're on your own now, responsible only to God for the way you do your work."

They responded well to the confidence I deposited in them. For some time everything went very well. Then one morning I came downstairs to meet a cluster of excited, round-eyed little girls.

"A sala de jantar dormiu aberto esta noite!", they cried out, in chorus. Quickly I translated to myself: "The dining room slept open last night!"

"Who was on duty?" I asked, speaking calmly.

"I was," Vittoria confessed, hanging her head and looking scared. "We were late to prayer meeting and I ran to go with the other girls. I meant to close the windows afterwards. Then I forgot until after I was in bed. I thought you'd find the windows open, and close them for me when you made your check."

"Well, Vittoria, I'm glad you told me the truth," I commended her. I looked at each of the other girls, then back to her. "Didn't I tell you all I'm not going to check on your work?"

They nodded vigorously, waiting to see what punishment I'd mete out to Vittoria, or perhaps to the whole group.

"I meant exactly what I said, and it still stands," I told them. "You can all be sure I shall not come behind you to catch you in a poor job, or in a lie. I'm not afraid, even though you left the windows open last night. After all, if a thief entered, he'd have to go through Dona Sophia's room and through your dormitory before he got to me! You see, girls, you and you alone are responsible for your work. Unless you do it, it will go undone."

As the girls said; *"Nunca mais a sala dormiu aberto!"* (Never again did the dining room sleep open.)

More important, I could see an increase in each girl's sense of responsibility, truthfulness, and feeling of personal worth.

Years later one of my dining room girls, now grown and married, laughed with me as we recalled that incident. She told me she never ceased thanking me for the lesson: the knowledge that she alone must be held accountable for any job assigned her.

Little did she know how keenly I recognized the dimension of my own responsibilities that day. However, I believe people usually try to live up to the confidence God or man, places in them.

She did, and so did I.

12.
Pioneer Work

IN FEBRUARY of 1895, Miss Watts and I journeyed to Petrópolis, the summer capitol of Brazil during the old Empire days, to open the new school there. What a magnificent location! Petrópolis built in a valley some twenty or thirty miles up in the mountains above Rio, is one of the most interesting cities I know. There was a little river that ran down the middle of the main street, and palm trees going on up into the mountains. Steep, winding roads curved upwards toward clusters of elegant marble and stucco houses. Beautiful!

Here is where the diplomats and their families retreated to escape the yellow fever in those days, before Dr. Oswaldo Cruz wiped out the disease. Rio expected a summer epidemic of yellow fever each year, a dreadful sickness that killed hundreds at a time.

The fever was of short duration, lasting only about seven days, but usually it was fatal. The Brazilians in Rio de Janeiro feared and dreaded it. They did not know that mosquitoes transmitted the sickness, but did know that they were apt to escape it if they'd catch the ferry boat at four o'clock each afternoon, cross the bay, and climb the mountain to Petrópolis for the night.

What they did not know was that the mosquito which transmitted yellow fever only flew from about four o'clock in the afternoon until two o'clock in the morning! If you stayed in Rio, you might get bitten, but if you summered in Petrópolis, you escaped the danger.

Our Petrópolis school, established only at the cost of much uphill, pioneer work, attracted the children of Brazil's ruling classes. We taught the children of Prudente José de Moráis Barros, Brazil's first elected president, and his brother, Manuel.

The new republic interested me mightily, of course. Its leaders and their children figured prominently in the establishment of our Protestant schools. Some of these Methodist schools, of course, began during Dom Pedro's reign as emperor, and I wondered just how significant a part they had played in influencing Brazilians toward their new republican form of government.

One thing I saw immediately was that the Brazilians esteemed Miss Watts, our first Methodist missionary to Brazil, almost to the point of reverence.

The Roman Catholics in Brazil did not welcome our influence at all. Many of the country's leaders, in a mood to cut all ties between church and state, had become disgusted with the Roman Catholic Church. As their mood shifted they became Protestant, but not necessarily Christian.

As they protested the Catholic hierarchy, the Pope and all "church interference", these Brazilians seemed to turn in our direction. Still, we knew that their rejection of the Pope did not necessarily spell acceptance of the Gospel of Christ as we taught it. While they patronized our mission schools and their children were trained there, they nevertheless did not always accept the Christian Gospel.

This was true of one of the men in the President's cabinet who wanted to put his children in school with me. He arrived one day when I was out, and when one of the teachers offered to matriculate his children he told her, "I don't want my children to study the Bible."

"In that case you'd better wait and see Miss Glenn," she told him.

The next morning he appeared with two handsome boys and a beautiful little girl in tow, all as smart as they could be. I showed him our course of instruction and he pronounced it satisfactory. I gave him the book so he could matriculate his children, and he said, "You know, I don't want my children to study the Bible."

"In that case, you'd better not enroll them," I said.

"Do you know who I am?" he demanded.

"Of course I do. You are the Minister of State," I replied.

"Well, I don't want my children to study the Bible."

"That's all right," I told him, "You have a perfect right to feel that way, but I tell you if they come to this school they *will* study the Bible. I have been sent here by a group of women in the United States for the special purpose of teaching the Bible. I could not refuse to teach it and be honest with them."

"You wouldn't teach my children to adore the Virgin Mary?" he asked.

"No, we honor the Virgin Mary as the holiest woman who ever lived, the mother of our Lord Jesus Christ, but we do not offer worship to her," I told him.

He continued to ask if we believed one thing and another, and ended by saying, "You don't believe in the infallibility of the Pope?"

"No," I countered, "and neither do you."

"I'm not talking about what you or I believe," he told me. "I'm talking about what you propose to teach my children."

At last, after we'd discussed every point, with those kids listening, he said, "Well, I'm going to matriculate them."

When he had finished the paper work, I told him, "If your children finish their full courses of study in this school, they never will hear as much discussion about the differences in one religion and another as they have heard this morning. We do not discuss religion with our children, we teach them the Bible. You say the Bible is the basis of your faith. I know it is the basis of mine. We teach the Bible and leave it to the children to accept and interpret it according to the light God gives them."

His kids stayed until they finished the course. They never joined the Protestant church, but they knew the Bible. I taught it to them.

Thus we established in Petrópolis a school whose fortunes inevitably were linked to those of the new republic. It interested me that Brazil had patterned its new Constitution almost exactly after the Constitution of our United States of America, and that they now elected their presidents, just as we elect ours.

My new work was among the most challenging I can remember. The children, some of the brightest, most talented sons and daughters of Brazil's leading families, were delightful to teach. However, we had little money and few workers in our new school, so I substituted at any job that had to be done.

In the classroom I became *professora* of English, drawing, mathematics geography, science, Bible and writing. I also supervised the dormitories and the recreation periods. Besides that, for six months I cooked three meals a day, until at last a cook was found who was not afraid to work for the *Protestantes.*

There was no Methodist church building in Petrópolis then, so our minister rented a large room above a grocery store for the purpose.

Miss Watts had a little old mutt dog that always went

95

with her to church, where she'd lie at Miss Watts' feet and give no trouble one way or another. Mrs. Hill, one of the English ladies there, owned a big Newfoundland dog which never came to church, but was kept tied up at home

One morning the Newfoundland got loose and found his way to church, arriving upstairs at our sanctuary while Mr Kennedy was praying. Of course Miss Watts' dog had to defend his premises, so the two got to fighting right over Mr. Kennedy's feet.

They made an awful racket. Mrs. Kennedy, our organist, sat on one of those old-fashioned stools, and as she pulled her feet way up out of the way of those dogs, that stool whirled around with her!

Since none of the men got up to throw those dogs out, Mr. Kennedy got up off his knees, took them by the necks, dragged them to the door, and rolled them down the steps. Then, believe it or not, he came back in, got down on his knees, and finished the prayer!

We were quite impressed with the dignified way Brother Kennedy handled the whole thing. Then he opened his Bible and commenced to read the Lesson, which began: 'Beware of dogs . . . " (Philippians 3:2).

We couldn't hold in another minute. We just whooped, even if we were in church. Brother Kennedy threw up his hands and said, "Brethren, it's right here in the Bible!"

I enjoyed my life and my work in Petrópolis. The little Sunday School and church above the store had much meaning for me. Membership grew to about one hundred for the Portuguese services, and probably seventy-five or eighty for the English ones.

It was easy to feel at home in Petrópolis, and I settled down to stay.

13.
New Responsibilities

WHEN I HAD worked in Petrópolis two years, the Board in Nashville decided to reopen the school in Rio, which had been closed when Mrs. Tucker resigned as its directress. After a period of local dissatisfaction and upheaval about which I knew nothing, Nashville headquarters had decided to close temporarily the Colegio Americano Fluminense.

Now the secretary in Nashville wrote to know if I'd be willing to brave the climate of Rio and the danger of yellow fever, to reopen the school. Remembering the institution I had visited when I first arrived in Brazil, and recalling Mrs. Tucker's generous offer to help me if the Board would consent to let me work in the school with her, I accepted the appointment. I knew I could expect the cordial help and cooperation of the missionaries at Rio de Janeiro, and the teachers at Fluminense.

Imagine my surprise and disillusionment, therefore, when I arrived in Rio to discover the Colegio virtually in a shambles!

Mrs. Tucker's successor had rented a rambling old two-story house and moved what was left of Colegio Americano Fluminense into this structure. There were nine double desks for adults, one old writing desk and chair, one dining table, six chairs, one *guardalonca* (cupboard), a tall iron hat rack, and, amazingly enough, the school's signboard, measuring two meters long and half a meter wide, with the name of our school painted across it.

If our worldly goods seemed meager, the friendly cooperation I had expected was perhaps even more so. Several days after I arrived, the Reverend Edward Tilly came to call on me. As he rose to go, he said: "Miss Glenn, if there is anything I can do for you personally, I am at your orders; but as for the Women's Board and their school, my hand is against them, now and always."

I could understand how he felt. Brother Tilly *was* provoked at the Women's Board for closing the school. Besides, he always liked to shock people by saying extravagant things. Nevertheless, I could not accede to his extravagance that time. I did not take the hand he proffered.

"I am here as a representative of the Women's Board to run a school," I told him. "If your hand is against them, it is against me. So you will excuse me if I do not take it!"

Shocked by my reaction, generous Ed Tilly immediately tried to make amends, but I did not shake hands with him

However, from that moment we understood one another and were allies, and he became one of my most faithful friends and co-workers.

This gives some idea of the atmosphere which awaited me when I came to Rio from my beloved Petrópolis. I had to build, somehow, a school to fit the *tableto* (Signboard) which bore the name of a defunct, discredited institution.

I plunged into the work. Ignorant as I was about such things, I realized it would be necessary to get a license for the school and advertise its opening.

I applied for the license at once. Meanwhile, I accepted five little American children as pupils, and soon several other children of the neighborhood came for matriculation. I also managed to secure a teacher who could teach Portuguese.

Things looked a little more hopeful, I told myself. Then, in order to license the school, an inspector came to check the house. He looked over the old building carefully, then reported it so full of termites it was *"capaz de cair em qualquer dia."* (Ready to fall down any day.) Instead of granting the license we needed, he ordered the little school closed at once.

It seemed a crushing blow. That day I started my long house-hunting trek which was to continue, intermittently, for twenty years. Our next move took us to a small house, which I rented for half the price I had been paying, from

101

a man vacationing in Europe. We lost most of our pupil in the move, but gained others in the new location. I se aside the rent money I saved with the intention of purchas ing desks later on. Thus I borrowed from Peter to pay Pau in order to establish some sort of little school.

A few months later the owner of the house returned, s we had to move again. A year later, we moved to a sti more commodious place which we had to lease for thre years. These strenuous, costly moves took their toll from my energies and the school's enrollment, but there seeme to be no help for it.

When we made that last move, received a license t operate our school, and hung the sign over our gate, decided it was time to take the big step. I spent the mone I'd saved from our rent economies on desks and othe school furniture, and hoped for the best.

When I reported to the Secretary of the Board in Nash ville on my action, telling how I had paid for the improve ments by economizing on rent, she wrote that I had n right to do any such thing. Since I had not used all my ren appropriation for rent, I should have reported the fact, anc not applied any of that money to any other object. Immedi ately she reduced my rent appropriation by one-half.

It seemed a bitter pill to swallow. I immediately mad a complete report concerning my handling of the missior funds, together with all receipts and vouchers, and maile these to her with my resignation, in case the Board was not satisfied.

"At least," I wrote, "my successor will have something to sit on when she comes!"

I received a quick and very conciliatory reply from the Women's Board in Nashville—but the reduction in the amount of rent was not changed.

I continued to request the restoration of the original amount, of course. Meanwhile, our monthly rent payments had to be met. We missionaries knew we were responsible for any debts of any nature that we might contract, and we could not appeal to the Board for any relief. That year I applied all of my salary, the entire $750, to the rent. My food was all the pay I received for my work that year.

Things looked dark, but my teachers all were devoted Christians who believed in prayer. We banded together and prayed that God would send us pupils enough to pay our current expenses. He did, and soon our school paid its own way. Eventually, I even got the rent appropriation restored.

This gives some idea of how difficult the housing situation became during the years I stayed in Rio. We didn't have any residence there, and I just had to rent and move from one place to another. I used to say I wished I was like a snail and could carry my house on my back.

One year we had a funny experience. I found a little old

house that belonged to some heirs. The man wanted us to take it over for the five years until the youngest heir came of age, when he could wash his hands of it. So we rented the little place.

I had doubled up with two other missionaries that year. They would stay with me in the house, and we planned to hire a teacher. Everything worked out fine—but the Board of Missions ordered me to close the place. There was nothing to do but go to the man from whom we had rented and ask him to take it back.

"Miss Glenn, you didn't know me, but I knew you," he said. "I don't want that place now for seven years. It's yours for that time, and you can do what you please with it. Sublet it, if you want to."

I didn't know what to do. I decided to sublet the place, and when I advertised it an Englishman who worked for an oil company looked the little house over and liked it. When he asked the price, I told him I hadn't the least idea of what it should be. I'd never had any experience with this sort of thing, and I just didn't know.

"Well, would such-and-such a price do?" he asked, and mentioned a sum. It was ten times as much as I would have thought about paying.

"Is it worth that to you?" I asked.

"Yes, of course."

"All right, the house is yours," I told him.

So I had that money. When the Mission Board wrote me

to close the house down, they reminded me that they were not responsible for my debts. I was on my own, and must make my own decisions about the house. Accordingly, I did not consult them about what to do with the unexpected income. I simply kept it!

Years later, I related the incident to two of our Mission Board officials back in the United States.

"You never reported that money!" one accused me.

"No, I didn't," I told her. "You refused to be responsible for that house at all. Therefore, I considered the income from it mine."

"She's got you there," the other board member remarked.

I had placed my membership at Catette Church, a quaint little edifice built during the Empire, when Protestant churches were not permitted to have bell towers. Except for the Anglican church, Cattete must be the oldest Protestant church in Brazil.

Now some of its members wanted me to take over direction of the Cattete School, a parochial institution sponsored by the church. Its sponsors had become weary of raising money to pay teachers' salaries, and there were other difficulties. Naturally, I stood aloof when the subject was discussed.

One day Brother Tilly came to the college to visit me, and asked me to take over the parochial school.

"My time belongs to the Women's Board," I assured

him solemnly, remembering our little tilt about the Board when I first arrived in Rio. "I can't possibly accept such a responsibility without consulting the authorities in Nashville."

Brother Tilly flared up immediately, saying they had nothing to do with the matter. However, I knew they did. I could see how, if I accepted the Cattete School responsibility, others would get out from under it. Eventually it would be passed to my successor, the Board then would become involved, and ultimately would become responsible.

I stood my ground, and Brother Tilly later saw things my way. So I simply wrote to the Board, asking permission to open parochial schools wherever feasible in connection with our Methodist churches in the city, which they granted.

We then held a formal meeting, and I placed before the parochial school board my proposition to charge a small tuition fee from which to pay the teachers' salaries.

"People appreciate what they pay for more than they appreciate charity," I argued. "I believe our attendance will be more regular and discipline will improve if we charge a modest tuition fee."

Finally the Board agreed to abide by my judgment—if I'd accept the responsibility. We advised the parents of the change, and few complained. Attendance and punctuality improved, and the school rapidly raised its standards.

I had already started a small parochial school in a private home at Jardin Botanica. I went to the parochial schools on Tuesdays and Thursdays, teaching Bible and mathematics. Other days I devoted to classes at the Colegio Americano Fluminense, where I had a corps of splendid teachers.

It seemed as though almost every minute of my life were taken up, but I could not complain. Our work grew and thrived, and we took enormous satisfaction in it. But for the sustained loyalty and devotion of my matchless staff, I could not have done what I did in my first five fascinating and often turbulent years in Brazil.

Then suddenly, abruptly, it was summer, 1899. My five-year mission to Brazil had ended. I took a furlough home.

14.
Money and Mosquitos

ORIGINALLY, Dad had objected strenuously to my going to Brazil. He hated to see me go; he was afraid for my health down there.

But when I came home on furlough, I found him not only resigned to the situation, but fully expecting me to return. By that time I felt so involved in the work that I couldn't let go. Dad knew this. He had become extremely interested in my work, and he wished me to continue my mission to Brazil.

Back in Rio, I learned I had been appointed Secretary and Treasurer of the women's work, in addition to my job of directing the schools. My new job was a big one, and when Bishop Wilson came I asked him to define my duties so I'd know exactly what was expected of me.

He showed me the paragraphs in the discipline defining the duties of the presiding elders, and said: "When the bishop is on the field his decisions will rule any case as to the location and supervision of the women missionaries and their work, just as he decides issues for the men and the general work.

"If any problem relative to the women's work should come up during his absence that cannot wait till the next episcopal visit, you must take the responsibility of making the decision in his place according to the rules laid down for the presiding elder, and report your action to the bishop and the Board.

"And you must give him all the necessary aid and information relative to the work of the women and their appointments of the women missionaries at Conferences."

I followed this rule to the best of my ability during all the years I served as Secretary-Treasurer—which was until World War I.

During many of those years, it was my duty to deliver the missionaries' salaries to them once a quarter. The cash for all our Methodist women's work was sent to me in one draft from the United States. I had to transfer the dollars into Brazilian currency and take that money in cash to wherever we had missions.

Everybody in Brazil had to carry money that way. I'd hide the money on my person and go out on one railroad stopping wherever I had to leave funds, then come back to Rio, pick up more money, and travel with it in another direction. Sometimes it took several days to deliver it all.

One day as I left for São Paulo a man came running

down the station platform and tossed into the window a package about a foot square.

"Will you please hand that to Dr. Sharman?" he asked me.

I put the package up in the hatrack. I had to change cars and take a little buckboard from my train to the other train over yonder, but fortunately remembered the package.

When I reached São Paulo at ten o'clock that night, I threw the packet on my dresser in the hotel, and went on to sleep. The next morning I left it there when I went down to breakfast, then came back upstairs, picked up the package, and took it down to Dr. Sharman.

"I don't know what this is, but somebody down in Rio tossed it in the window and asked me to deliver it to you," I said.

"I know what it is," he replied. "Thank you so much."

He reached in his pocket and pulled out a pair of scissors. (I never knew a Brazilian man to carry a pocket knife, but they all carry little old blunt scissors.) When he cut the string and the paper fell away it was greenbacks!

"Well, listen!" I told him. "I don't know *who* that man was, but I know *what* he was. He was a fool, and you can tell him I said so!"

"He knew who you are," Dr. Sharman said.

"I don't care," I said. "You write that man and tell him never to do a thing like that again. If he does, he'd better

111

follow the train right on down the track, because I'll toss his package out the window."

"You wouldn't do that," Dr. Sharman objected.

"I'll do it!.," I promised him. "There might be a dozen men in that railroad train who would guess what that was and knock me in the head to get it."

It never occurred to me to be afraid of being robbed. I never did look like a millionaire. I dressed very, very simply and never wore jewelry and a whole lot of stuff. Nevertheless, it was a great relief when in 1913 the National City Bank of New York established a branch bank in Rio and advertised that they'd issue checks.

Everybody predicted they'd go broke in less than a year. By that time, however, the bank was doing nearly all the financial business back inside Brazil, so other banks had to offer the same services. It was a relief to be able to deal with checks!

The change in banking practices all but revolutionized Brazil, I thought, but before that happened something even more remarkable had changed the life of my great new country: Dr. Oswaldo Cruz had tracked down and gotten rid of yellow fever!

When Brazil put old Dr. Cruz in charge of the Health Department, he organized a health corps they called "the mosquito killers". This corps of men went from one street to another, inspected houses for any kind of water deposit, used kerosene on any container of water they saw lying around, and they wiped out yellow fever absolutely!

I had come to respect yellow fever. Though I never contracted it, I nursed my share of cases. Many of our girls and some of the missionaries caught the fever, and quite a few died. I never lost any I nursed, luckily, though people died like flies during the summer epidemics in Rio.

One old doctor, an American missionary, treated the sickness most effectively. He hardly ever lost a case. He had a special prescription which he gave to me, and I still have it somewhere in my things.

If you caught yellow fever, you were expected to die. Most did, within the week. When one of our missionaries came down with it I wrote her brother in the United States, saying, "If, when you receive this, you have not received a cablegram saying she has died, you may know she's on the way to recovery." Fortunately, I did not have to send the cable.

Maidee Smith, one of our missionaries, came very close to dying with the fever. Maidee was a real musician, with the loveliest voice I ever heard. This talented girl became gravely sick.

"If you can make her rest quietly tonight, you might save her," the doctor told me, "otherwise, there's no chance of it." I sat beside Maidee, trying to soothe the tossing, moaning woman. At last she spoke.

"Sing to me," she whispered. "If you sing to me, I can go to sleep."

What a strange request! "Honey, you know I can't sing," I protested.

"Yes, you can!"

I couldn't believe she wanted me to sing, but she insisted, so there was nothing to do but sing. I sat beside her, stroking her hand, and I sang. The minute I'd quit singing she'd grab my hand tightly and whisper, "Sing on."

I sang every hymn I knew the tune and verse to, and the moment I'd quit she'd grab my hand again. I sang all night long. That sounds like a lie, but it's a fact. The next morning, Maidee had passed her crisis, and she soon got well.

I took care of all our missionaries when they got sick. I also taught all day long, and directed all our schools in Rio de Janeiro, too. I don't know how I did it, but I did.

Our parochial schools sprouted all over the city, wherever we established churches, and I supervised them for the teachers. These were graded schools, founded on the American system, but of course taught in Portuguese. Some accommodated only twenty-five to one hundred pupils, others as many as two hundred or three hundred. Our school system took boys and girls alike.

I also had Bible class with all my teachers and taught them how to study the Bible. Together we reorganized the Bible courses we taught in our schools.

Meanwhile, our Colegio Americano Fluminense entered into a period of prosperity, and soon was full to the limit. Our pupils came from the outstanding families in

Rio, including the members of the presidents' cabinets, leading doctors, lawyers, educators, military and navy men. These men's sons were trained in our schools, and later became leaders of Brazil.

So our work prospered and was a blessing to all involved in it. The years seemed full, full to the brim, and they fairly sped along.

Before I knew it, America became implicated in World War I. Back in Georgia, my parents had become old and ill, and needed me.

I saw it was time to go home.

15.
Journey Home

THE BOARD didn't want me to resign. They suggested that I take a long vacation with pay, but I couldn't do that. It wouldn't have been honest. I didn't intend to go back into mission work as long as my father and stepmother needed me.

As it turned out, I stayed home for five years, and resigned for that period. My service in Brazil was to span forty years, but I worked only thirty-five of them.

Because of the war, America needed people who could translate Portuguese. They could get Spanish, German and anything else, but seemed like they couldn't get Portuguese translators. They kept writing to me from the U. S. Bureau of Censors in New York to come work there, but I refused.

"Now listen," my father ordered at last. "None of the boys has been able to get into this fight. They're all too busy with war work.

"So if there's anything in that lingo you got out yonder

that will help win this war, you go on. We'll get along somehow."

I arranged with two great-grandnephews to stay with Dad and Mother at night, and I went to New York and worked for the censorship bureau. The job lasted about a year.

It was very interesting. We had to read and censor everything that went backwards and forwards about the United States and the war, and when I'd done that a while I caught up with a spy ring that was working against the United States.

How did I catch them? The chief censor asked me how, and I didn't exactly know; just instinct, I guess.

The spies were smuggling their messages in on blueprints. As a child, you remember, I'd coaxed my brothers to teach me to read blueprints, for no special reason, and they did.

Something about these prints just didn't make sense. I got suspicious because a group of prints, which obviously should have been a set, was mailed piece by piece. Scrutinizing them carefully, I noticed that from Print A to B to C to D, the word written under "A" followed by the word written under "B", and so on, gave a complete message. When you put one sheet on top of another, in proper sequence, you could read the message.

I took the blueprints to the chief censor and asked if he

saw anything suspicious. He looked them over carefully, but found nothing amiss.

"Look at them this way," I suggested, and showed him what I had discovered. He saw it immediately. From then on, every letter addressed to the man who had sent the blueprints, or coming from him, had to be brought to the chief censor. Eventually they caught up with the spy, and prosecuted him. I received an official commendation from the United States Government for my part in the matter.

When I returned to Georgia, I went to work for the *Conyers Times* Publishing Company as an assistant editor and feature writer. The work suited me fine, and I enjoyed every minute of it. Meanwhile, Dad and Mother required more and more constant supervision, and I was grateful to be able to take care of them.

Dad died in September, 1922, at age ninety-one. Mother was old too, I realized, and her health was failing fast. One of my brothers took Mother to Chattanooga to spend the winter with him. He had a centrally heated house, and felt she could be more comfortable there with him than she could with me, in our drafty old place.

Mother went up there and got sick, and without asking my leave or anything about it, just wrote that she was coming, and to meet her at the train.

"Mother, I thought you were going to spend the winter," I said when I met her at the train.

"Peg, I'm sick," she replied. She still called me by my childhood nickname, Peg. "If I'm going to be sick I want to be with you."

"That's all right, Mother," I told her. "I want you to be."

I took care of Mother as long as she lived—until Christmas Eve of that same year. She must have been about seventy.

Suddenly, my once-almost-too-full life seemed nearly empty. I had fewer responsibilities, I thought, than I ever had known before.

What should I do? Where did the Lord intend to lead me next?

Hardly could I ask the question, it seemed, before His answer came.

I received a call to return to my beloved Brazil.

16.
New Call to Brazil

"I WANT TO GO back to Brazil, if I can do any good at all," I told the Women's Board, "but please don't give me a whole lot of responsibility."

I'd had a hard time in the United States, working at the Postal Censorship Bureau, and so on. Anyhow, I was beginning to get along in age.

"Don't worry that I have any foolish notions about not being able to work under some younger women,"I told them. "I'll gladly take any work you offer me, just so I don't have the prime responsibility."

But that's not the way it turned out. The younger women out there had come in under my direction, and none wanted me under her! So instead of my working under one of them, they assigned me to head the Central Mission in Rio, which was a place for indigent hill children—the hardest place going! I had asked for an easy place, but they gave me the hardest.

Well. The mission settlement was built on a hill in the

slums of Rio, a place called the Hill of Thieves. It included a clinic for expectant mothers, a baby clinic, a Methodist church, and a school.

I reached my post just at the end of the school year. You never saw such a lack of discipline in your life. You couldn't hear yourself think!

I wasn't in charge. The woman in charge was a mighty fine person, but she was not a disciplinarian.

When they appointed me head of that institution for the next year, I called a teachers' meeting. I meant to try to instill in everyone the necessity for discipline.

"Miss Glenn," they protested in dismay, "you don't know these children! You worked with upper-class children before now. These children are different. They are homeless, and have had no training."

I could not agree with them.

"Listen, children are children the world over, no matter whether they come from a king's palace or where," I insisted. "They need somebody to discipline them, and they love discipline if you can get it into them."

I had three weeks in which to convince those folks of the necessity for the discipline in which I so strongly believed. I had the strength of my convictions, so I rammed it in and crammed it in and jammed it in!

"I will not be here as a whip," I told them. "You can call me and I can come into your room and settle any question that arises. I can make the rebellious child apologize to you and to the rest of the class. But when I walk out, discipline walks out with me—and he knows it.

"Consequently, you must expect that when you say a thing, it's going to be done. Demand that it be done."

I can't say they were all convinced at first, but I worked with them until it sank in.

When school started the following fall, we took simple steps to turn the rowdy, riotous schoolhouse into a quiet, mannerly place of learning. The first day of school, each teacher stood in the school yard and allowed her children to line up behind her in single file. When I stood at the head of the steps and clapped the bell, they marched in and took their seats.

Immediately a sense of order began to prevail. The kids got so they were quite proud of it. Why, they'd yank one another into line. Soon there was real discipline in that school, and it's going on yet. We got that uncontrollable school so well lined up that when the Superintendent of Public Instruction visited, he asked permission to bring the Normal School girls (student teachers) down there to see what discipline meant. We let them come.

My teachers became convinced that these kids were no different from the wealthy ones. The children's self-respect increased. They became proud of their discipline and kept it going themselves.

I think perhaps the most important work I did in Brazil was that of getting the teachers to accept their responsibility to carry on their work. We had started many schools in Rio and elsewhere. Each had its own principal, but I had taught in most of them at some time, had trained many of the teachers, and had supervised all the schools.

As I got older I became conscious that I could not supervise those schools forever. I had to know they'd be carried on, and that standards would remain high. It was time for the Brazilian teachers I had trained to assume the responsibility. They had to control the children. I remember the time I had trying to get them to understand that they could control the children.

Our experiences with the Central Mission did just that. It became a model school, and my Brazilian teachers have carried its work forward in fine style to this day.

More and more, I wanted to see the Brazilians take over the work of the Methodist Church in their country, and they did. Soon after my return to Rio, we organized the Women's Missionary Society in Brazil. They wanted to make me their first president.

"Absolutely no!" I told them. "This is your society. You must elect your officers from your own women. You must make your own plans. You must realize you've got to do the work yourselves and you've got to support your projects without any help from the United States."

They took up the challenge, and did just that. The society we organized then, with about fifteen splendid women, grew until today they are sending missionaries to

Portugal. The Society, which formed in São Paulo, has spread throughout Brazil.

One thing you have to realize, as we talk about the spread of the faith throughout Brazil, is the time in which we were working. The forty years I spent in Brazil were embraced in the half century that saw the most tremendous changes that have come to the world, as well as to Brazil. The scientific changes, moreover, were no more marvelous than the social, moral and spiritual changes that took place.

That's especially true in relation to the standing of womanhood. You women of today, with your complete freedom to vote, hold office, study for any profession, and to go and come when and how you please, might find it hard to imagine the circumstances of women's lives in Brazil when I first came to that country.

No respectable Brazilian lady ever went out on the street unless she was accompanied by her father, brother, husband or son. Lacking one of those escorts, she had to take even a small servant boy. It had to be someone with britches on!

For that reason, Brazil's street peddlers thrived. From door to door, they sold merchandise of every description —from sumptuous silks and satins, embroideries and threads, to the wares of the lowly fish vendor.

As we American missionaries had no husbands or brothers on hand to escort us, and didn't always realize the

125

implication of going out alone, we simply came and went as business or inclination required. Without knowing it, we managed to blaze the trail for our Brazilian sisters in their march toward more freedom.

This did not come at once, of course, either in Brazil or in America. The handful of Brazilian women who met to form the Women's Missionary Society, for example, were those who lived close by the American missionaries. Other women were not free to go out on the street in order to attend such a meeting—and that was in 1923!

Alas, while I rejoice in modern woman's freedom, sometimes I think it has gone a bit too far. Brazilian women once didn't go out on the street unless they were accompanied by someone wearing britches. Now they wear the britches themselves!

And so, of course, do the women of America.

17.
Instituto Anna Gonzaga

GOD SAVED the happiest work of all for my last years in Brazil.

I had come to realize that one of the big problems in Brazil was that nobody did any menial work. I felt they needed almost more than anything else to learn to honor honest work, to learn to do it well, and to be proud of the fact that they could earn a living.

A school, I thought, would be the answer—a vocational school for children.

I had no money to establish such a school. Then I met Dona Anna Gonzaga, an old maid who was outrageously wealthy. She had inherited a large fortune from each of her parents.

Dona Anna Gonzaga and I became good friends, and she gave me her mother's farm, which amounted to about 1,300 acres of land with 50,000 orange trees on it—a magnificent gift.

I was overjoyed. The land had been divided up into tenant acreages of several-acre parcels, each with a small

127

shack. Rentals from these tenants came to me, and I took over two of those small holdings and established a new orphanage. We started out with fifteen children, and put the boys in one of the small houses, the girls in another.

As you can imagine, the houses were in bad repair. My childhood training on the plantation became useful here. Fortunately, I had learned to saw and align, and to drive a nail without mashing my fingers. Soon I was repairing the little houses, teaching the boys to help me, and together we built sturdy furniture for both cottages, using packing boxes for lumber.

We named our new orphanage-vocational school the Anna Gonzaga Institute. Dona Anna, however, didn't live long enough after that to see much of our dream come true. She fell, broke a hip, and died soon afterwards. I went on and opened the school as I knew she wanted it, and it's a fine memorial to her today.

The Anna Gonzaga Institute also became a real memorial to my own parents, in a way. I decided that these children would live as a family, and they'd grow up, as far as possible, the way Dad had raised our big family. I'd try to make them self-sufficient, yet interested in others. They'd need to learn to make their own decisions, chart their own courses, yet work together for the good of all. Also, I determined, we'd have the sort of fun we kids had known in our home.

There was a lot of work to it. These were poor children,

all dependent. We started out with six girls and seven boys; our oldest, a boy, was fifteen.

One of our tenant farmers had set up a dairy. He knew nothing at all about dairying, but thought he could live in town, let his cows graze, have someone milk them, and that would be all there was to it. When his dairy failed, he asked me to take the cows as payment of his debts.

"I might take over two, if you have two good ones," I agreed.

"They're very good cows," he assured me. "They give more than a half gallon of milk a day!"

"If they can't give more than that I can fatten them and sell them," I thought. I took two. I milked one and taught Pedro, our fifteen-year-old, to milk the other.

We went to the English mill and persuaded them practically to give us their bran chaff for cattle food. Soon we raised our milk production to four or five times as much, and had all the good milk and butter we needed.

Since I churned every other day, we had a lot of buttermilk. "What a shame these kids don't know how to drink this good buttermilk," I thought. The Brazilians didn't drink buttermilk.

I knew they wouldn't drink it if I told them they had to, so I did what I wouldn't allow any teacher to do. I brought a jar of buttermilk and put it at my place at the table. One of the little girls couldn't bear to see anybody have anything she didn't have. When she saw me drinking

129

that she said, "Miss Glenn, is that good?"

"I think it is," I told her. "I don't know whether you'd like it or not. Do you want to try it?"

"Yes'm!"

She brought her glass, and I put in just a little bit. "You can try it, and if you like it you can have some more," I said, "but it's too good to throw away."

She tried it. "That's *good!*"

"I think it is," I agreed. Then of course every kid had to have some, and soon they all drank buttermilk.

The boys learned to garden, and we raised much of our own food besides the milk, butter and buttermilk we got from our two cows. We raised chickens, too, but mostly the kids ate a Brazilian dish called *arroz e feijados* (rice and beans), which they loved. We sliced dried beef, soaked it, boiled it, then cooked it with rice and beans. The result was something like the Hopping John we southerners eat on New Year's Day.

One thing we did (and I think I thought it up) was to make a cooler. We had no electricity or refrigeration, of course, and I invented this thing through necessity.

I took a large goods box, removed the top and bottom, put shelves in there, and then tacked burlap across it. I made a shallow wooden box which went on top, filled that with water, and the water seeped down through the burlap and kept things inside just as cool and nice!

When the Superintendent of Public Instruction inspected our school, he was amazed at the contraption and had to have an explanation. He had arrived in a critical mood. We were *Protestantes*, and I could see he meant to condemn wherever he could.

Soon the superintendent was carrying on over our neat store of fresh milk and butter, kept so nicely in the home-made cooler. He never had seen anything else like it.

As I showed him around my kitchen, he asked, "Where do you do your cooking?"

"Right in here," I said, and he couldn't believe me. You see, the Brazilians had no idea about closing up the top of a stove. They'd just let the smoke come out until the inside of their kitchens looked like the inside of a stove chimney. My kitchen, however, was clean and nice as could be.

"Where do you boil your rice and beans?" he asked, staring about in disbelief.

"Right here," I repeated. Then I explained. "I know what you're thinking, doctor, but we use the flue of our stove to carry the smoke up. We cook our food on top of the stove." He never had seen anything like that before, and he seemed impressed.

After I showed him the stove and cooler, it was time to display the cows and the place where we kept them.

"Doctor, now I must show you what I know is against the law," I told him. "The law in Rio says we must have a cemented space for our cows to stand on so we can wash them off. But I can't afford a cement space. Besides, I don't

131

think it's healthy. I've seen cows stand on cement until their hooves turned up. It's cruel!"

The superintendent followed me outside without comment. We had placed our cow lot back of the house, over the rise of the hill, and I'd had the boys haul sand to spread over the lot. We dug a pit just outside the fence, and we threw all the droppings into that pit, covered it with leaves and dirt, and made compost. He inspected the arrangement without comment.

"Yonder are our cows, over there in the pasture, with a clean branch of water so they can get all the good water they want," I offered. Still he said nothing.

"Miss Glenn," the superintendent said at last, "if I report this I've got to say it's against the law. So I just won't report it." And he never did.

When we got back to the house I took some oiled paper and wrapped up one of our blocks of butter and said, "Please take this to your wife, with my compliments."

"Oh-h-h-h! Won't you let me have two kilos of this good butter a week?" he asked.

"Why, no! I couldn't!" I told him. "If I did, I wouldn't have enough butter for my children."

Now the superintendent really looked astonished. "You mean to tell me you feed those children this butter?" he asked.

"Of course. That's what I make it for."

He glanced out the window to where my children were

playing, and I followed his eyes. The English-speaking people in Rio gave me their old clothes, handsome goods, which I'd rip up and use to make suits for my kids. I taught the older girls to sew, and we really kept the lot of them very nicely dressed. They all looked cute!

"Hmph! You call these children orphans?" he asked in a tone of some disgust. "Why, they look better than my own children do, this minute!"

The Instituto Anna Gonzaga required me to work from dawn to dusk, but we had time to do everything we needed to do. We had several teachers, but we all lived as a family more than stressing the school atmosphere. We had time to know the children individually, and to teach them all sorts of things—cooking, sewing, housekeeping, farming, repair work—the skills I'd learned as a child in Georgia.

We divided the kids into groups. One group worked in the kitchen and helped provide the food for a week, another worked in the dormitory and kept the house, and a third took care of the laundry. Each group had a teacher to encourage and help them, and chores were rotated weekly.

We worked closely together, and enjoyed one another. One day the Board of Directors met out there, and one of the men took an orange, peeled it off and dropped the peeling on the ground. Immediately one of my little boys ran for the trash box, picked up the peelings, and told the man, "Miss Glenn doesn't allow us to throw garbage on the ground."

The man looked right much ashamed, then laughed and said, "I think I'll come out here and join your school."

Each night we had story-telling time, just as we did at home when I was a kid. My kids took turns telling stories before we had Bible reading and prayer prior to bedtime. At the breakfast table, after the meal was eaten and everybody had taken their coffee, we'd read a Bible passage and have prayer before we went about our separate tasks.

Always we took our meals together, and lived as a family. We served sensible, well-cooked meals and taught the children how to act at the table. We taught them to speak up and share anything pleasant and nice they had to tell.

I gave them a lot of love. We did all the things I did growing up with Dad and Mother, and I tried to establish the regime Dad used so successfully. I wanted the children to become proud of their ability to control themselves and to make their own living. I tried to make each one able and willing to make his own decisions, as our father had done for us. I tried.

I taught them the Bible verse, "I will guide thee with mine eye" (Psalms 32:8), and I controlled them with my eyes. I never did spank a child, and I never had one I could not control. I've never seen one I couldn't control.

Years later, when I returned to Brazil, I found that all

of these children, except one, turned out very well indeed. I grieve for the one who went wrong. I loved her and all the others very dearly, and they loved me.

The Anna Gonzaga Institute flourished and grew. In the half century since I established it, hundreds of children have gone through that school and grown into happy, successful adults.

The Anna Gonzaga Institute meant as much to me as any other single thing I managed to begin during my thirty-five years in Brazil. It has a special place in my heart.

18.
Retirement

I RETIRED in 1934. I didn't ask to—they just retired me. It was time! I had come to Brazil forty years earlier. Now sixty-eight and growing somewhat deaf, I was thankful to accept the Mission Board's retirement salary and come on back home.

It seemed hard to realize I had spent more of my lifetime in Brazil than I had in my own United States of America. I loved the Brazilians, and loved Brazil. It was hard to leave them.

Still, I returned to America with my sense of adventure running high. "What will the Lord send now?" I wondered as I looked ahead.

Always I look ahead. I try to find out the Lord's will in my life, and I devote my life to His service. That's why I really don't like the word *retire*. As long as God keeps me here, I figure He has work for me to do.

I came home to Conyers, Georgia to find out what that work might be. Eventually I went to the *Conyers Times* office to see if I could get my old job back. The *Times* had a new editor. He said he intended to move the office in a few weeks, and would need some help then.

"Listen, if I'm going to help you then, I'd rather come on now and help with the move," I argued, "That way, I can put things where they're to be, and learn from the beginning."

"That would be all right," he agreed. "When can you start?"

I looked around and saw a nail on the wall, so I took off my hat and hung it on the nail.

"I'm ready," I told him. So I started to work.

There were many things to do in Conyers, which is one of the nicest little towns in the world. I taught Sunday School, just teaching the Bible as I had done for so many years. I joined the Women's Society for Christian Service and attended all those meetings. Often I went as a delegate to meetings as far away as Portland, Oregon. I love to travel.

When I retired, I bought a four-room house in Conyers, and I enjoyed keeping house for many years. It was easy to walk from there to anywhere in town—to church, the post office, newspaper office, or any of the meetings I wanted to attend.

Sometimes my kid brother, Mark Twain Glenn, would come from his home in St. Petersburg, Florida to visit me. Twain is my half brother, born when I was a twenty-one-year-old school teacher out here in the country, and he's the only other one of Dad's kids besides me who still survives.

Mother (my stepmother and Twain's mother) had three babies, but her other two boys died in infancy. We loved little Mark Twain, and spoiled him outrageously. He always has said he had two mothers, my stepmother and me, and he knew which one he had to mind!

I was strict with him. He could bend Mother around his little finger and persuade her to do anything. I insisted on his doing the right things. He could have his play things and play with them, but when he got through he must pick them up and put them away.

I gave Twain a little old wash stand that had a place where he could store his things. One day he had a half-gallon bucket of big hickory nuts he loved to play with, and he'd strewn them all over the floor. Some little boys came and called for him to play with them, and I said, "Pick up your hickory nuts first, Hon."

"Let him go on. I'll pick them up," Mother said.

So he went on.

"Mother, you'll hear from that," I warned.

"No, he'll never remember it," she said.

The next time he played with his hickory nuts and they needed to be picked up, I said, "Hon, pick up your hickory nuts."

"Mama will pick them up," he told me.

139

Mother got a little switch and she switched him—the only time I ever saw her do that! She was very tender hearted.

Twain, of course, was named for the author Samuel Clemens, who used the pen name of Mark Twain. When my brother was about three years old, I had his picture taken and sent it to Clemens with a letter written to sound as though little Mark Twain wrote it. I never expected to hear from him, but quick as the mails could go and come back, here came a good-sized photograph of Clemens addressed to little Mark Twain Glenn, complete with a letter saying he hoped his namesake would avoid making the many mistakes the author had made!

It's a lovely little letter, and is one of Twain's precious things.

With so much to do, the years sped by. I was past ninety when we took on the project of restoring the old Mount Tabor Methodist Church, the one I'd attended all those years long ago with Dad and Mama, and where my grandfather preached. If I hadn't actually been born in the second pew of that church, I told people, I reckon I did grow up there!

But the church had gone down to nothing. One day I dug out my grandfather's old membership list for Mount Tabor, and mailed it to the *Atlanta Constitution*. I asked the newspaper to print the list, with an invitation to all descendants to come together at old Mount Tabor one Sunday in August.

When I went out to see the old preacher, he said we needn't count on him. He only came to the church one Sunday a month, and that wouldn't be his Sunday.

Well, those descendants came. The woods were full of them! Everybody brought lunch, and we had dinner on the grounds. Even the old preacher showed up and ate with us. After dinner, they asked me to speak. My niece, who remembered hearing her mother talk about old Mount Tabor Methodist Church, had sent me twenty dollars.

"I didn't call you all here to take up a collection, and I don't intend to take up a collection," I said, "but when I wrote my niece and told her about our getting together, she sent me this money.

"This money doesn't belong to me. It belongs to Mount Tabor. I'm putting it on this table, and if anybody wants to put anything with it, they can do it."

They just fell all over themselves. When they finished laying money on the table, it amounted to two hundred dollars.

"Why, there's enough to repair this old church!" I said, and they all agreed.

"Well listen. It's laying-by time," I pointed out. "Why couldn't you all come here and do this work yourselves?"

The men all looked at one another, and finally they said they could.

"All right now," I told them, "Come on here tomorrow and do it!"

They did. They got together there and fixed up that old church. Some fellows from Atlanta took to going all the way down there and working on it. With so many toiling they got it back in repair. Then they commenced to have Sunday school every week and preaching on a regular basis. They remodeled it and fixed it up and put new pews in it. My parents would be very pleased to see what all they did to the old place. I was, myself.

Besides my trips and travels, my work (I just *don't* accept the word *retire)*, and a constant stream of visitors to my little house in Conyers, I kept up the largest amount of correspondence you ever saw.

Writing letters is a lifetime habit with me. I keep up with more people than you can shake a stick at, and I have done so for years. Postage remains a major expense for me.

I have friends all over the world, and some are hand-me-downs from one generation to another. For example, Miss Schaeffer and I were missionaries together out yonder. She came home, and I visited her in Trinidad, Colorado.

She and I wrote together until she got sick and died. Her sister Rose took up writing to me while Miss Schaeffer was sick, and afterwards Rose and I corresponded for years on end until Rose died. Her brother George took over and wrote and wrote and wrote till he died, and now his niece Margaret and her husband continue to write to me. Someone once figured I must average writing and receiving about a thousand letters a year! I really don't know.

As I got up into my nineties, I began to plan toward entering the home for retired missionaries at Asheville, North Carolina, which is run by the Women's Society for Christian Service. It seemed a good idea to go there, except for one thing—the many long distance phone calls I'd be obliged to make to all my friends back in Conyers!

Then a wonderful thing happened. The North Georgia Conference of the United Methodist Church commenced to build one of the most remarkable modern retirement centers in the United States, right there in Atlanta. It's one of those apartment houses planned for older people, a gorgeous place that looks just like a luxury hotel.

I was ninety-nine years old when I applied for admission to Wesley Woods, and the retirement center was brand new. I asked to see Mr. Scott Houston, Jr., the director.

"Mr. Houston is out of town today. May I help you?" a nice young lady asked.

"I reckon so," I told her, and went on to explain that I hoped to move to Wesley Woods. I made the mistake of telling the young woman my age, and she advised me that I'd better wait until their new health center was built the following year.

I began to get her drift. She thought I was too old to live alone—that I probably was sick, and needed attention. Why, I hadn't been sick in bed in more than twenty-five years! She didn't know that, of course. How would she know that I did all my own work, and took care of myself?

"Can you touch your toes, young woman?", I asked her.

"Why, no-o-o-o."

"Well, I can!" With that I backed away from her desk and proceeded to do a few toe touches, just so she could see I was still able. It seemed to impress her. She suggested that I wait for Mr. Houston to return, and apply to him.

In a few days, I saw Mr. Houston, and he accepted my application. I moved into one of the most interesting worlds in which I ever have moved, filled with fine people retired from every kind of profession you can think of. Several other former missionaries live in the apartment towers here. Our friends call those of us who served in Brazil "the Brazil nuts."

I fixed up my room with some of my favorite things. There are family portraits on the wall, Grandpa Glenn's writing desk he used as a missionary to Florida, a glass fronted bookcase filled with Dad's old books and Mama's four-volume Bible, the books I used at Scarritt; and then there's my electric typewriter, on which I write my weekly newspaper column, which for years I have contributed to three local newspapers. Oh, there's just an accumulation of things I've saved for a hundred years and more. It's home.

At Wesley Woods, where I'm the oldest resident, they've made me into something of a pet. I tell my friends they spoil me till I'm rotten, then complain because I smell!

My friends not only put up with me, but treat me wonderfully well. Truly the Lord has blessed me with a collection of marvelous friends!

19.
My New Century

IT'S WONDERFUL to become a hundred years old! People make a world of fuss over you, and go to lots of trouble. When it happened to me, my friends arranged the most eye-popping surprises you ever heard of in your life.

They arranged to send me back to Brazil for a visit. Can you imagine a more thrilling gift? I was elated!

Mr. Scott Houston, Jr. took a three-week leave from Wesley Woods in order to accompany me. My kid brother, Mark Twain, now seventy-nine, decided he'd come along too. Twain never had seen Brazil.

I started writing my friends down there, and they got ready for us. One of my old schoolboys, by then a retired admiral, telephoned the Brazilian Embassy in Washington, D. C., and asked them to roll out the red carpet for his old teacher. I made an itinerary of the places I just had to see; all my old schools, if possible, the Instituto Anna Gonzaga, and dozens of friends.

This would be my third trip to Brazil since I retired in

1934. In 1949 I returned for the first time. In 1955, when they invited me to attend our twenty-fifth anniversary observance of the founding of the autonomous Methodist Church of Brazil, I used funds I had laid up for my burial expenses to pay for the trip. I was determined to go! My Brazilian friends had quite a laugh when I told them how much I was enjoying my "funeral procession"—much more, certainly, than if I were actually dead!

In 1956 the Brazilian government awarded me, through their Embassy in Washington, D. C., the highest medal Brazil can bestow—the Order of the Southern Cross. President Juscelino Kubitschek presented the award to me in appreciation for my service to Brazil. I esteem it highly, and always wear the handsome decoration when I attend any big affair where Brazilians will be.

My one hundredth birthday celebration actually started two days early, with a marvelous party at the Conyers Methodist Church. The whole place seemed to overflow with friends, flowers, smiles and hugs—and such a cake!

I rode into the second century of my life on a huge tide of visitors, greetings, letters and flowers. March 8 whirled by like an exciting dream: a television interview . . . a drive to the State Capitol, where Gov. Carl E. Sanders came out to the car to wish me happy birthday . . . the flight to Washington, D. C. with Twain and Mr. Houston . . . our arrival at Dulles International Airport in Washington, with the entire Brazilian Embassy staff there to meet me . . . the ambassador's limousine and liveried chauffeur, which he placed at my orders while I was in Washington!

That limousine even took me to see my own president. My congressman, Representative James A. Mackay, had arranged for me to visit the White House, and he took me to meet President Lyndon B. Johnson.

Mr. Johnson concentrated on a thing before him to the exclusion of everything else. As we entered his office he must have seen us, but he paid no attention. He was reading a document, and went on reading it until he was finished. Then he made an annotation on it and turned to us with a bow.

The President received us graciously, and presented me with a medallion with his likeness on it. I apologized for interrupting the multitudinous duties of the most important man on earth, just to give me the honor of seeing him.

"The honor is mine, Miss Glenn," he said gently.

"Mr. President, I'm nothing but a poor white school teacher from the South . . ." I began.

"Just like me," President Johnson said, and took my hand.

"Mr. President, now that I'm here I want to tell you that I pray for you daily, by name."

"I need your prayers," he responded.

"I have the same promise you have," I continued, "the promise that 'But they that wait upon the Lord shall renew their strength and shall mount up with wings as eagles.

149

They shall run and not be weary, they shall walk and not faint' "(Isaiah 40:31).

President Johnson listened attentively as I spoke; his eyes are very expressive. "I've reached the walking stage, Mr. President," I concluded,"but you're still in the flying stage. God bless you!"

I liked President Johnson. I thought him a fine man, and very thoughtful. When I got home from Brazil I found he had sent me a color photograph of the two of us, made during our visit, which he had inscribed. The picture now hangs in the Wesley Woods lobby.

In New York I became the first one hundred-year-old to land in a helicopter at the new Pan American Building in Manhattan, a thoroughly enjoyable experience. Later we toured the Methodist Board of Missions, then appeared on radio and television interviews before we enplaned for Rio de Janeiro.

Air travel is wonderful! How marvelous to fly from New York City, U. S. A. to Rio de Janeiro, Brazil in just twenty-two hours, I thought, remembering that long, twenty-three-day first journey by boat in 1894.

I remember each day of our three weeks in Brazil as among the most exciting of my life. My friends out did themselves. They gave us a red carpet reception. Everywhere there were orchids, speeches, official greetings and welcomes, newspaper stories—and my own little speeches, spoken in the Portuguese I discovered I still remembered!

Our travels seemed to be one long hero's welcome. It was a red letter day when I returned to my well-loved Anna Gonzaga Institute, where the children greeted me with songs and gifts and kisses. I felt an overwhelming sense of love and happiness as I went from familiar school to church to city to friend, enjoying the visit that seemed only too short.

Everywhere, friends received me with love and honored me with ceremonies. There were assemblies at the schools . . . welcomes from Methodist church pulpits . . . official receptions by Brazilian government officials, including President Castelo Branco . . . visits with governors and mayors . . . a standing ovation from the legislators when I was introduced in the House of Representatives . . . .

Each day presented its own special thrills. Mr. Houston and Twain seemed to have just as big a time as I did, although they were plagued a day or so with some little sickness. I dosed them, and they perked up and enjoyed the rest of the trip. I didn't get sick a minute.

Can you imagine a happier climax to a happy life?

I can't. The good Lord blessed me with the world's best friends, I decided, as we whirled through my beloved Brazil, swept along by laughter, hugs and kisses.

20.
Time

I'LL NEVER retire. At 103, I figure I'll just go on doing as I please, and the good Lord keeps showing me interesting things to do.

Each day is an adventure. I wake up about half past five in the morning. I say my prayers then, do my exercises, take a bath, and dress for breakfast.

After each meal, I lie down for about fifteen minutes. Then I go to work, reading, or writing, or whatever I want to do. What time I go to bed at night depends altogether on how I feel. If I'm working at anything, or writing one of my newspaper columns, I may sit up until eleven at night, or later. If I've had a hard day or feel tired and let down, I just flop and go to sleep as early as seven. Then I may awaken around midnight, to read, or think, or take out my pad and write. I do some of my best writing in the middle of the night.

I still like to travel, and I visit my friends all over this big state. I attend prayer meetings, church conferences, and still speak in Methodist churches throughout Georgia on behalf of foreign mission.

A Christian doesn't get too old to praise the Lord, I decided. As long as I live, I mean to serve Him the best way I can—and I must say, that keeps life interesting.

When I returned to Scarritt College, now located in Nashville, Tennessee, to address the 1966 graduating class, I shared with them my feelings about time. Today, three years into my second century in this world, I still live by this philosophy.

> *A hundred years is a long time on anybody's calendar, and I am amazed as I think how our Lord has allowed me to share in so much of His most precious gift to man - for I consider time God's most valuable gift to the world. He considers it so important that He deals it out one second at a time, and every thing, and every creature on earth must share that small second.*

> *The king on the throne is granted no more of it than a prisoner in the dungeon. The millionaire in his mansion is given no more of it than the poorest beggar on the street. The wisest scientist is granted the same amount that is given to the idiot. The chemist in his laboratory has no more than the boy flying his kite. It can neither be bought nor sold. The miser cannot hoard it. Even the most generous soul cannot give it away. The bird singing on his leafy perch has just as much of it as a farmer sowing his seed or following his plow.*

The richly attired society leader must share it with the poor seamstress that stitched her laces. The president of Harvard must share it with the most ignorant bushman in Africa. The most noted evangelist is granted the same amount as the vilest sinner. The wise man and the clown share it alike.

This instant is yours, and it is mine. What will we do with it? We can only use it or lose it. Which shall it be?

Longfellow very fittingly says:

> Art is long and time is fleeting,
> And our hearts though stout and brave,
> Still, like muffled drums, are beating
> Funeral marches to the grave.
> Let us then be up and doing,
> With a heart for any fate;
> Still achieving, still pursuing,
> Learn to labor and to wait.

If I had to go back over my life, I don't know of a single thing I would change. I tried to decide honestly and to establish firmly my decisions, and I never regretted any of them.

Dad taught us to make our own decisions and stick by them, and I think that is the guiding principle more than any other that has influenced my character.

Looking back, I see how early the hand of God touched

my life, too. Everything in my early childhood pointed me toward the path God meant me to take, and prepared me for a life in His service.

Just as I did not realize that my happy, happy childhood on the Yellow River plantation in Georgia would prepare me for a life's work on foreign missions, I had no conscious knowledge of becoming a Christian, as I know now a Christian should be; I think that just gradually grew on me. I was not a true Christian when I joined the church. I joined as a girl of sixteen, just because it was the thing to do; it was after that, that I fully realized the Christian attitude toward life.

Teaching school helped bring this about, and my children taught me in this respect. I well remember how one small boy taught me a lesson in faith.

When I was about fifteen, a cyclone had come along and blown the roof off our house. My father and mother were away from home at the time, and it scared the wits out of me. After that, every time I saw a cloud as big as my hand I'd fly to shut the window.

If a little weather blew up at night, I'd stay awake. If a little wind came up I'd go in Dad's room and sit on the side of his bed until Dad drove me out.

"You're just losing your grip on yourself," he'd scold me. "Go on back yonder and go to bed!" He'd make me go. But I wouldn't stay in my room. I'd go on into the boys' room and crawl in bed with them. They were fellow sufferers, because they had been with me the night of the storm.

Even when I got to teaching, when a storm came up I'd almost lose my head. One day when I was teaching out at Klondike, a pretty stiff wind came up and scared me to death. I walked up and down the room, until finally I realized I had to control myself or I'd lose control of the children. I went and took a seat. One of the little boys came running up to me, dropped to his knees, put his elbows on my knees and looked up into my face.

"Miss Layona, you scared?" he asked me. With the storm going on, I didn't dare lie and say, "No"!

"Willie, don't you know the Lord will take care of us?" I countered his question.

Now there was the thing. To this day I can't tell you the difference between believing and knowing. I couldn't honestly say "I believe He will," but I said, "I know He will."

"If you ain't scared, I ain't either," Willie said.

He got up and went right back to his little seat and sat down. I never prayed harder in my life. I remember I literally prayed for the Lord to stop that storm. And it *stopped.* Those trees that were bowing clear to the ground straightened up, the wind ceased, and the rain stopped falling. I needed to see that. Thanks to Willie, the Lord cured my fear of storms.

There were many others like Willie. Although I never married, my life has been filled with children. God placed the solitary in families for the purpose of training children.

Maybe the Lord kept me solitary because He knew I was going to have all those children.

How many? Only the Lord knows!

I have asked the Lord to direct everything I did, and I tried to follow His directions. People sometimes ask me if I ever had any crisis that He took care of in Brazil. I tell them I had a crisis every day!

I also had indescribable rewards. One great joy was that the Republic of Brazil established freedom of religion. In this climate, our work could flourish. Side by side, we Methodists worked with missionaries from the Presbyterian, Episcopal and Baptist denominations, too, and gradually even the tensions between Roman Catholics and Protestants disappeared.

The idea of ecumenism began and flourished there in our beautiful Brazil long before any of us knew what the word meant. It just came about as the result of practical Christianity at work.

When you live to be one hundred, people tend to ask you to what you attribute your longevity. I tell them I'm accustomed to following God's will, and He evidently still has work for me to do.

I believe He does. Looking back, remembering, I marvel at God's goodness to me. I don't believe I know another 103-year-old lady anywhere who feels any happier, or who has been more richly blessed!